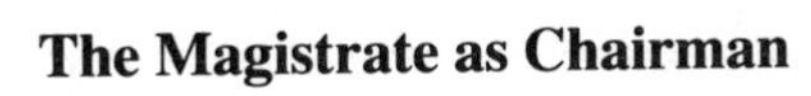

The Magistrate as Chairman

The Magistrate as Chairman

Enid Ralphs CBE, JP, DL, BA
Vice President of the Magistrates' Association

Geoffrey Norman JP, MA (Oxon), Solicitor
Lord Chancellor's Training Officer

With a foreword by
The Rt Hon The Lord Denning, DCL

Published by Butterworths in association with
the Magistrates' Association
London
1987

United Kingdom	Butterworth & Co (Publishers) Ltd, 88 Kingsway, LONDON WC2B 6AB and 61A North Castle Street, EDINBURGH EH2 3LJ
Australia	Butterworths Pty Ltd, SYDNEY, MELBOURNE, BRISBANE, ADELAIDE, PERTH, CANBERRA and HOBART
Canada	Butterworths. A division of Reed Inc., TORONTO and VANCOUVER
New Zealand	Butterworths of New Zealand Ltd, WELLINGTON and AUCKLAND
Singapore	Butterworth & Co (Asia) Pte Ltd, SINGAPORE
South Africa	Butterworth Publishers (Pty) Ltd, DURBAN and PRETORIA
USA	Butterworths Legal Publishers, ST PAUL, Minnesota, SEATTLE, Washington, BOSTON, Massachusetts, AUSTIN, Texas and D & S Publishers, CLEARWATER, Florida

Ralphs, Enid
The magistrate as chairman.
1. Police magistrates — England
I. Title II. Norman, Geoffrey
III. Magistrates' Association
344.205'12 KD7309

ISBN 0 406 10469 7

Typeset by Lin-Art, Ashford, Kent
Printed and bound in Great Britain by Biddles Ltd, Guildford and Kings Lynn

To Anne and Helen

Foreword

I ought to know as much as anyone about the Chairmanship of a Bench: because I presided over a Bench of Judges – the Court of Appeal – for over twenty years. The phrase – 'Bench of Magistrates' – is derived from the same historical origin. The 'Bench' was in early times a long seat, usually of wood or stone, with or without a back, on which three or four judges used to sit to hear argument and give judgment. But that was five hundred years ago. Nowadays no-one sits on a Bench. Every judge or magistrate sits on a chair. The one who presides over a Bench of Magistrates is the Chairman. They sit usually as three. That is quite the best number for any court. The Chairman sits in the middle. He has *in law* no greater authority than the others. His vote counts no more than theirs. He is simply *primus inter pares* – the first among equals. But he has *in fact* much greater authority and correspondingly greater responsibility. He ought to be – and usually is – more experienced than those who sit beside him. He ought to be – and usually is – more knowledgeable in the law and practice than they. He takes the lead in any discussion. In case of difference, the others usually defer to him. Most important of all, it is he who gives the judgment of the court. He speaks for all.

So I am glad to commend this book about Chairmanship. It is concerned especially with the Chairman, and about him. It is written by Lady Ralphs who was herself one of the best of Chairmen I have ever met. She was until recently the Chairman of the Council of The Magistrates' Association. She has written it jointly with Geoffrey Norman who was until recently the Secretary of the Association. You could not have better sources of information and instruction. Any royalties are to go to The Magistrates' Association of which I am an Honorary Member. So it gives me especial pleasure to write this foreword for it.

Although I ought to know as much as anyone about

Chairmanship, I have never put it into writing. This book does it. It puts it into writing and does it exceedingly well. It makes me feel like M. Jourdain who had been speaking prose all his life without knowing it. So I have been acting 'Chairmanship' nearly all my life without knowing it. You will recall the classic passage from Moliere's *Le Bourgeois Gentilhomme:*

> *M. Jourdain:* What? when I say: 'Nicole, bring me my slippers, and give me my night-cap,' is that prose?
>
> *Professor of Philosophy:* Yes, Sir.
>
> *M. Jourdain:* Good heavens! For more than forty years I have been speaking prose without knowing it.

So here: many of the hints and much of the advice come as second nature to me. I have known them all my life. But there are significant differences between the Chairmanship of a Court of Appeal and the Chairmanship of a Bench of Magistrates. Such as that on a Bench of Magistrates 'Questions are put through the Chair'. One or other of the magistrates hands a note to the Chairman or whispers to him suggesting a question and the Chairman decides whether to put it or not. I entirely agree – for a Magistrates' Court. But in the Court of Appeal my colleagues would have none of it. Some would virtually take charge of the questioning and do it themselves. Whilst I, like Brer Rabbit in the Uncle Remus stories: 'He lay low and say nuthin.' I would just interject at the end, 'Perhaps we can move on to another point.'

Another piece of advice given by the authors is that a majority decision 'must never be disclosed as such'. That may be all right for a Bench of Magistrates. But in the Court of Appeal my colleagues would not stand for it. Nor would I. If I dissented, I said so, loud and clear. I have often told the apocryphal story: 'When I was a judge of first instance sitting alone, I could and did do justice. But in the Court of Appeal of three, I found that the chances of doing justice were two to one against' – with me being the one dissenter.

Then there is the difficulty about the giving of reasons. Every court in the land and every tribunal is nowadays expected to give reasons – except in the most obvious of cases. But not a Magistrates' Court. Throughout my time magistrates never gave reasons. They went by the advice which Lord Mansfield is said to have given to a subordinate judge: 'Give your decision but never give your reasons: for your decision may well be right, but your reasons are almost certain to be wrong.' In that respect magistrates are like juries. A jury does not give reasons. So it is difficult to upset their verdict.

Likewise with magistrates. If they do not give reasons, it is difficult to upset them.

But this book tells us differently:

There is a growing feeling that the bench should usually include reasons . . . We are convinced that all chairmen in every one of our courts, held in over six hundred petty sessional divisions, could collectively enhance respect for law and order by the dignity, confidence, clarity and humanity with which they pronounce sentence.'

I agree, but it needs a chairman of high calibre to be able to do it. And suppose he makes a mess of it? The last state of that bench will be worse than the first. So it all depends on the Chairman. If he reads this book – and follows its advice – he will come out on top.

Then there is the vexed question of the relationship between the Chairman of the Bench and the Clerk. Years ago I knew of some clerks who used to dominate the proceedings. They would ask questions of the witnesses. They would argue with counsel. When it came to a decision, they would retire with the Bench and tell them which way to decide. Lord Goddard in a famous case put a stop to all that. It is all gone, thank goodness. This book gives us the modern practice. The senior clerks have many courts to attend to. They have to run a complicated administrative machine. They are not able to sit in every court or on every case. They have to leave it to junior clerks. This means that the Chairman takes on his proper role. He presides with authority and knowledge. He only asks the Clerk occasionally for advice when a difficult point of law arises. I would recommend to every justices' clerk the advice given to us as children, 'Don't speak until you are spoken to.' In other words: When the Chairman asks for your advice give it, but do not intervene unless you are invited to do so: except in the rare case when something occurs to you on the law in which you think your advice would be helpful.

Then the book brings us up to date on topics of all sorts. In my time the magistrates had no power to punish disruptive conduct. Proceedings were sometimes brought to a standstill. The offenders might sometimes be removed from court but that was no deterrent. But now under the Contempt of Court Act 1981 the court may order the offender to be kept in custody until the rising of the court: and may commit him to custody for one month or impose a fine of £1,000 or both. That is very light compared to the case in the *Year Books* which I delight to recall in the Norman-French. When the culprit was sentenced:

'Il jetted un brickbat a le juge que narrowly mist.'

It is said that the judge had his head aside on his hand as the brickbat whizzed past, and straightening himself up, he said: 'If I'd been an upright judge, I should no longer be a judge.' He ordered the man's hand to be cut off!

As I read this book, I was impressed more and more with the great importance of our Magistrates' Courts in our judicial system. They already deal at one stage or another with about 98 per cent of all criminal cases. They may soon be given more jurisdiction over more minor cases which are better tried by them than by juries. In every court, the Chairman plays a key role. It is extremely valuable to have this book devoted to him: but it should be read by every magistrate also, because it deals with so many facets of his work: and all done in such a readable style. Just as *Stone's Justices' Manual* is essential in every courtroom and lawyer's office, so this book, *The Magistrate as Chairman* is essential in every Chairman's study or on his desk.

Denning

January 1987

Preface

This book is offered to all who occupy the chair in magistrates' courts. It attempts to include all facets of their task. It refers to statutory and case law where necessary but its focus is on the responsibilities and rewards of chairmanship as well as the problems and pitfalls.

Balancing the scales of justice in the presence of witnesses, clerks, advocates, defendants and probation officers, under the public gaze, is not always easy. Challenging and worthwhile it invariably is. The object is to ensure the smooth and efficient running of the court, to highlight excellence, suppress irrelevance and distraction and secure the proper administration of justice. We hope this book will help those faced with this task to fulfil it and add to their satisfaction in it.

Enid Ralphs
Geoffrey Norman
March 1987

Acknowledgements

We thank the friends and colleagues who, knowingly or unknowingly, have contributed to this book.

In particular we are deeply indebted to Mr Derek Howard, Deputy Secretary of The Magistrates' Association, for his unfailing encouragement and support. An author himself, his comments were as invaluable for the text as was his experience in bringing the book to the point of publication under the auspices of The Magistrates' Association.

This was facilitated by decisions taken by the Honorary Officers of the Association, Dr Douglas Acres, Chairman, Mrs Margaret Romanes, and Mr John Hosking, Deputy Chairmen, Lord Ingrow, the former, Mr Jeremy Langton the present Treasurer, and the Executive Committee. Their generous support has added immeasurably to the pleasure of our task.

We were fortunate in colleagues, with unrivalled experience of the work of Justices of the Peace, who read and challenged the text. They included Mrs Rosemary Thomson, Chairman of the Training Committee of The Magistrates' Association, Mr Ronald Horsman, Editor of *The Magistrate,* Mr Basil Scott, Deputy Secretary of Commissions, Lord Chancellor's Department and Mr George Whiteside, Clerk to the Chertsey and Woking Justices.

The publishers and authors wish to thank the following for permission to reproduce material as indicated:

The Berkshire Branch of The Magistrates' Association for their guideline of matters to be considered when deciding guilty or not guilty and sentence (in Appendix IV)

The Training Committee and Training Officers for the East Midlands Region for the form of procedure before magistrates' court for bail or custody (Appendix V)

The Leicestershire Constabulary for the form of application for remand in custody/conditional bail (Appendix V)

N J Stephens, Esq, Clerk to the Justices, Bath, for the checklist for magistrates' search warrants (Appendix VIII)

Contents

Appendices

Chapter 1

Introduction to chairmanship

'I seem to have taken on a full-time job,' said a chairman-elect after a training course on chairmanship of the bench. Certainly it is a fulfilling task which takes time. Time to do and time to master.

He has also taken on a vital judicial role. He will imprint his individual hallmark on the courts over which he presides. For many of those who appear as witnesses or defendants in the magistrates' courts, it will be their only contact with the system of criminal justice. The impression it makes will be reflected in their subsequent attitudes to law and order. This involves everyone who takes the chair in a magistrates' court, whether as bench chairman, an elected deputy, or chairman for the day.

For some new chairmen the task is daunting. For most experienced chairmen it is a job they undertake conscientiously and with a confidence born of training and practice. Every magistrate is a potential chairman. Chairmanship is nevertheless a speciality in which excellence is of paramount importance. All good justices are not equally fitted for this particular task but those who do not take the chair are not relegated to the role of the supporting cast. The bench is essentially an entity and a wise chairman values the presence of colleagues to whom he can turn for sound, balanced and independent judgment.

INDUCTION TO THE CHAIR

The current work load of benches means that many justices will be called upon to act as chairman for the day. Some, with previous experience of presiding in other spheres, can undertake this earlier than others. A course in chairmanship, and two years' experience on the bench, are recommended before taking the chair. These years are of the utmost preparatory importance. Throughout their duration an individual's acuteness of observation of the conduct of the court and depth of perception of the decision-making process will emerge. Both are necessary qualifications for chairmanship.

Becoming a chairman is not a terminus. Experience is of great importance and to the wide awake and receptive every sitting should continue to add knowledge and skill. Chairmanship is a process of learning rather than a state of having learnt.

Because experience is important, it is understandable that age and length of service on the bench are often equated with qualification to take the chair. It has been emphasised that selection should be according to suitability rather than seniority. To achieve this objective the early testing of potential is provided for. An elected chairman may sit aside for a colleague to take the chair.[1] This can be a halfway house on the way to full chairmanship. Guilty pleas, or cases in which a statement of facts has been served and a written plea of guilty received, are appropriate for this purpose. This initial experience should help in the evaluation of qualification for chairmanship whether in others or ourselves.

It is important for the chairman, in consultation with the justices' clerk, to ensure that, as far as possible, the inexperienced sit with the experienced, whether justices or court clerks. Part of the preparation for chairmanship lies in hearing all types of cases and in participating in every kind of court. Newly appointed justices should not find themselves regularly relegated to the apparently 'easy courts'. Breadth of experience at the outset of a magistrate's career will help him appreciate the importance of every court decision.

ATTRIBUTES AND ATTITUDES APPROPRIATE FOR CHAIRMANSHIP

Contrived judicial attitudes are as transparent as they are futile. The bench performs a judicial task which demands integrity, insight and dignity in execution, if it is to command respect.

The scales of justice symbolise the balance which is the key to the

1 The Justices of the Peace Act 1979, s 17(2) enables an elected bench chairman or deputy chairman to invite another justice to preside over the court in his presence in accordance with r 9 of the Justices of the Peace (Size and Chairmanship of Bench) Rules 1986, SI 1986/923, as long as he is satisfied as to the suitability of that justice for that purpose.

magistrate's task; a balance between the protection of the public and the proper claims of the defendant in mitigation. It often appears that victims of crime are paid scant attention in contrast to the offender, who has many agencies to assist him. Over the years the due process of law has supplanted private vengeance. A public which may not take the law into its hands rightly looks to the court for protection.

This protection incorporates the rule of law as the foundation of the liberty of individuals and the stability of society. Liberty has many facets and is relative. It is upheld in our courts. Both the protection of our rights and our duties, relevant to the proper claims of others, are enforceable at law. The chairman's perception of this balance can help less experienced colleagues to apply its principles.

It goes without saying that the chairman should be of good standing, not only in the neighbourhood but among his colleagues. He should be able to communicate with them in his judicial, training and personal capacities. The last is important because a good chairman may well become the confidant of some colleagues whose private circumstances precipitate problems which complicate judicial duties. Others may ask questions relevant to their task. Others again may have faults and failings which, if tackled early, can be eliminated to reveal admirable justices. Moreover the chairman should be sensitive to diffidence. For those colleagues in whom this quality reflects an awareness of the responsibilities of office, a little encouragement from their chairman may ensure the survival of a good justice who might otherwise have turned back.

A chairman should be an example of neutrality in dress. This is all the more necessary because we do not wear the self-effacing robes of the judge which centralise the function rather than the individual exercising it. Club or regimental ties, badges and the like should not be worn in court as they give rise to a suspicion of bias. While funereal black and covered heads are not a necessary adjunct to dignified court proceedings, dress should be appropriate and unobtrusive. This applies to officials and advocates who appear before the bench as much as to magistrates. Chairmen should therefore ensure that those who come inappropriately dressed are discreetly advised of the fact before they make a second appearance.

The chairman should arrive early in the retiring room and be equally conscientious about punctuality in opening the court at the appointed time. The magistracy is voluntary, not only in the sense that it is unpaid. Every justice decides for himself whether or not to undertake its duties. Once committed, no personal predilection or convenience should deflect him from his magisterial obligation.

APTITUDES FOR CHAIRMANSHIP

It is easy to detail the personal qualities which should prohibit, retard or expedite the journey to the chair. Among the prohibitions are those which should inhibit a person from becoming a magistrate in the first place. They have caused more than one honourably to resign, often having admirable qualities more appropriate to other spheres of activity.

The chairman needs the psychological stamina to arrive at a conclusion, stand by it and act on it knowing the reward of such single-mindedness may be public criticism to which no personal response can be made. Such criticism usually comes through the press or the media.

Magistrates hold a public office. It is right that the discharge of this office should be subject to public scrutiny. Sometimes adverse comment is made ahead of the necessary insight or information. If it is justified, the court should modify its future decisions accordingly. Having given his full mind and all his powers to his task at the relevant time, a justice should try not to relive, in subsequent doubt, decisions judicially taken. Justices need to know how easy it is to identify with human weakness and human wickedness. This facility is good when it deepens understanding but a hazard if it clouds judgment.

Is self-importance an occupational hazard of magistrates? If so, slow progress towards taking the chair may be both a cure and a consequence of the affliction. It is possible for a justice, overwhelmed by the importance of his office, to feel that a bit of it has rubbed off on to himself. No person in court should be a humbler servant of the law than the justices themselves. What graver responsibility can there be than sitting in judgment on others? Reputation and liberty are at stake. The whole future life of the defendant may be influenced by the outcome of his case.

Individuals have a range of attributes, some unsuspected by themselves, which are capable of development. Certain qualities are essential in a chairman.

Chairmen must be fair minded; intellectually fitted to follow an argument and underline the points salient to decision; able to conduct a court with calm, courtesy and dignity; able to make it clear who is ultimately responsible for its control and able to exercise the necessary authority.

Detachment can be more difficult to attain. All of us have prejudices arising out of our particular experience. We have therefore to cultivate sufficient self-examination to neutralise them in our judgments. The overriding responsibility is to apply the law and to interpret accurately the will of Parliament. Lord Denning pointed out: 'If a judge or a magistrate should say "I do not agree with this statute or regulation and therefore I will inflict a nominal penalty", he would be doing a grievous wrong.'[2] It is well to be warned by the chairman of the bench who, in 1949, described an Act of Parliament as 'a very evilly worded Act' and a 'most disgraceful Act' and imposed a nominal penalty of one shilling. He was removed by the Lord Chancellor.[3]

Any enthusiasm for the purpose of a particular statute or disappointment at its limitations should not be reflected unduly in the penalty we impose. Application and experience can foster detachment. Magistrates have to be able to cope with the occasions, albeit infrequent, when they are confronted with the undisguised face of evil. Anger must be controlled, even when dealing with offenders responsible for the repeated and callous exploitation of others, particularly the young, the weak and the poor, for gain or self-gratification. Such conduct is not new to an experienced chairman. He can contain and restrain the natural repugnance of less experienced colleagues which may spill over, in the privacy of the retiring room, into unacceptable displays of anger and, subsequently, stringent, appealable sentences.

Another necessary quality is patience. Patience to hear anything and everything relevant to the case and presented according to the rules of evidence without, by tone of voice or gesture, indicating frustration at the slow pace of the proceedings.

Among helpful qualities can be a sense of humour. This often engenders a sense of proportion. Though there is no laughter on the bench, there is occasionally a smile, at any rate in the retiring room.

THE RESPONSIBILITY OF OFFICE

The chairman's responsibility is formidable. For the majority of defendants, for family and friends who accompany them, and for the public who observe, experience of the judicial system of the country will be confined to the magistrates' court. The impression given of the whole system will to a large extent be created by the chairman of the bench. Towards them he will turn the face of justice at a potentially sensitive and impressionable time in their lives. If they go away feeling that the proceedings have been efficient and expeditious without being hurried and the trial has been fair, these

2 See Kenny, 'Judicial Behaviour'.
3 Justice of the Peace at 345. (1985 149.)

feelings will be, in no small degree, attributable to the chairman's conduct of the court.

Nothing we have said is intended to imply that there is a stereotype chairman or that it is desirable to mask individual style, personality or gift. Goals should be held in common but there is no single route by which to reach them. Just as the bench should reflect the community which it serves so the differing attributes of chairmen reflect the individuality of fellow citizens and, properly controlled, inspire confidence in our common humanity.

Chapter 2

The chairman in court

It is frequently pointed out that around 98% of all criminal cases begin and end in magistrates' courts. Quantity impresses. Quality counts.

The chairman must establish the authority of the bench. This should be exercised firmly but with restraint. He will have to see to it that the dignity of the court is never at risk. The orderly and efficient conduct of the business of the court is – and should be seen to be – in his (the chairman's) hands. The clerk is there to advise and full use should be made of his professional skill, but it is the chairman, speaking for the whole bench, who gives rulings on points of law, decides on the arrangement of the business and announces the decision of the court. In all these matters he will, whenever necessary, consult his colleagues and the clerk. The chairman's leading role in court requires an alert and confident manner and the ability to speak at the right time without being prompted.[1]

THE ENTRY

Chairmen should ensure a punctual and purposeful entry into court. If justices file in, in the order in which they will sit, this allows the chairman to take his central seat without any undignified re-shuffling in the public eye. Before he does so, in many courts, he bows in acknowledgment of a similar greeting from the court. It is no matter whether the inclination is from the neck or the waist. This may indicate no more than the flexibility of the anatomy in

1 *Handbook for Newly Appointed Justices of the Peace*, Lord Chancellor's Department, 1984.

question! In either case, it should be unhurried and unselfconscious. It signals the orderliness and courtesy with which the day's business will be conducted, and the fact that the chairman has approved the start of the day's list. The clerk can then call the first case. An alternative, as soon as the bench is seated, is for the clerk to ask permission to call the first defendant or for the chairman to give it unsolicited.

Few attributes are more destructive of the judicial attitude than self-importance. Superficially there may appear to be some temptation in this direction. Justices look important. They sit higher than everyone else. They are greeted with ceremony and addressed with deference. These rituals help maintain dignity, and by putting distance between the participants in the proceedings, they centralise the essential function of the court, namely the administration of justice. Ritual makes for smooth running by rendering the proceedings predictable. Each participant knows his part and place.

THE OATH OR THE AFFIRMATION

Custom, once established, can be adapted to meet the exigencies of a particular situation. Its adaptation should take place under the watchful eye of the chairman, always vigilant as to the conduct of the court. In our view it is preferable that the clerk or the usher should administer the oath. The statute[2] is impartial as to whether the uplifted hand is the right or the left. The chairman may have to intervene if a conscientious usher is insisting on the customary right hand, to the further confusion of an already apprehensive witness.

Unnecessary intervention should be avoided. The normal practice is to proceed with the administration of the oath unless and until the witness objects. He is not obliged to state the grounds of his objection. Once objection is made, the person must be allowed to affirm.[3] The Oaths Act[4] states that 'The officer shall (unless the person about to take the oath voluntarily objects thereto or is physically incapable of so taking the oath) administer the oath in the manner aforesaid without question.'

The chairman should give the defendant or witness his full attention as he takes the oath. He can do much to ensure that it is meticulously administered and properly taken whether on the New

2 Oaths Act 1909, s 2(1).
3 *Stone's Justices' Manual* (1987), para 2-418.
4 Oaths Act 1978, s 1(2).

Testament, the Old Testament, the Koran, the Granth or in accordance with unfamiliar ethnic procedures, if he maintains silence in court. This silence at the outset of his evidence may help the witness to appreciate the gravity of perjury.

RELATIONSHIPS IN COURT

Order in court depends largely on the chairman, who controls it through his relationship with the clerk, the advocates, the duty solicitor, the defendant, the witnesses, the police, the probation officer, the public and with his magisterial colleagues. In court the link is functional rather than personal.

With the clerk

This requires a chapter on its own (chapter 3). The best introduction to it is summed up in the word 'partnership'.

With the advocates

Advocates merit respect. At times they require patience. The chairman should be wary of trying to hurry them. They are professional people with a case to make and a duty to present it. Their clients must feel that it has been put fully before the court. Moreover, the chairman should avoid, as far as possible, any intervention which might undermine the confidence which should properly exist between a lawyer and his client.

Nevertheless, there is a limit to the number of times the same point needs to be made without some reassurance from the chairman that it has been taken. Chairmen have to ensure that all evidence is relevant to the case. As so often, a question is preferable to a rebuke. A tactful enquiry as to where a particular line of enquiry is leading will generally bring an explanation or a change of course. Very rarely, a chairman may have to intervene because of the harassment of a witness. Occasionally a witness feels harassed by an advocate who fails to make his question comprehensible. It may then be helpful for the chairman to intervene with 'I think you are asking. . .'.

Listening is not a passive state. The chairman must be alert and critical to ensure that no liberties are taken with the rules of evidence. Intervention has to be swift to prevent such harm being done that the hearing of the case has to be adjourned to be heard before a different bench. Usually a chairman's knowledge and experience will be a sufficient guide on hearsay evidence. He will understand the reasons for excluding it because it was secondhand, it was unsworn, and there is no opportunity for the cross-examination of the person who gave it. He may need guidance from the clerk as to its admissibility if it comes under an exception to the hearsay rule. Leading questions (ie questions which are so worded that they suggest the answer) – such as 'She was wearing a red jacket, wasn't she?' – are inadmissible in examination-in-chief. Nevertheless, with the clear agreement and acquiescence of the parties, an exception to the rule can sometimes be made. If the chairman fears that an infringement of the rules has occurred, he can always instruct a witness not to answer until he has sought the advice of the clerk.

The chairman should subject the closing speech for the defence to continuous analysis to ensure that no new material, unsupported by evidence, is introduced. The adversarial nature of the proceedings requires the chairman to maintain the fairness so carefully protected by the rules of evidence.

Unfortunately, the proportion of experienced advocates appearing in magistrates' courts has dropped. The example of the experienced can be the best training in adversarial skills, the presentation of facts and the courtesies necessary to retain the dignity of the court. If courtesy is lacking, a word to the clerk to the justices, to be conveyed informally to the person concerned, is often all that is required and is gratefully received.

Advocates are subject to considerable pressure in court. Any apparent discourtesy, such as late arrival, usually prompts an apology and explanation. Sometimes it occurs because cases overlap in two courts. This delay is inevitable from time to time. It should not be tolerated where it occurs because an advocate has accepted instructions on too many cases listed on the same day and in different courts. The clerk may suggest privately a sharing of his load with other advocates. Despite concerted efforts, delays in getting cases heard persist. They are, occasionally, protracted by advocates. A chairman should make sure the bench knows the reasons for any application for adjournment before it is granted. If the reasons were avoidable, the chairman should make an appropriate observation. Avoidable delay is not in the interests of justice. The bench should always be able to answer the question, 'Why?' to its own satisfaction before granting an adjournment.

Before court, efforts are made to save professional time and conserve the legal aid fund, by sorting the day's list so that defence advocates deal with their business sequentially. Sorting the list is a complex matter, particularly in a busy remand court. The chairman should be on the look out for any further helpful adjustments which may prove possible during the course of proceedings.

With the duty solicitor

The duty solicitor is available for the otherwise unrepresented defendant. The chairman should make sure that an unrepresented defendant knows about the duty solicitor. Anyone who wishes to see him can get help with legal aid and with bail applications as well as advice on his plea and mitigation. He may be told of rights which he did not realise were his, such as to apply for an adjournment to trace a witness.

With the defendant

The defendant is the reason for the court case. He should be made to feel by the demeanour and attentiveness of the bench that his case is as important to them as it is to him, albeit for different reasons. It is important to distinguish between the defendant and what he is alleged to have done. This involves no compromise with the implications of crime. The court should never further diminish the defendant's dignity. One way to avoid this is to address the defendant formally as 'Mr Jones' throughout the proceedings rather than 'Jones' or 'William Jones'. The equivalent for women as between Mrs and Miss may involve some research. The risk of a mistake is worth taking.

Except for the announcement of decisions, the chairman does not address the represented defendant directly without reference to his solicitor. If the defendant attempts to speak to the bench, he should be asked to give his instructions to his advocate. Defendants may try to disrupt court procedure. Some outbursts, for instance on a refusal of bail or on sentence, can be ignored, unless couched in insulting language. They are a personal emotional reaction. Insults, on the other hand, have a target and merit the procedure for contempt.

If intervention is necessary, it is important to act resolutely but not to over-react. The smile on a defendant's face may be a sign of nerves or insolence. The chewing of gum can be an involuntary comfort or an act of defiance. The defendant may not be conscious of the whereabouts of his hands, or he may dig them into his pockets as a deliberate gesture of contempt. Co-accused, separated by remands in custody and on bail, may respond to a meaningful hint from the chair that a reunion conversation in the dock is not in order, before the seriousness of the proceedings underlines the point. The correct interpretation of conduct is vital to any decision about intervention and the manner thereof. Offence should not be taken where none is intended and a defendant should be given an opportunity to correct or apologise for his conduct before a contempt is punished.

The accused has the right to have his case heard fully. He may try to intervene from the dock, not knowing that procedure allows a proper place for his side to be put; or for his solicitor to take instructions when he feels his case is being inadequately presented. An explanation of procedure from the chairman may be enough to still his concern. However, any danger of a defendant disrupting or dominating proceedings has to be dealt with by firm warning followed by action.

It is important for the chairman to distinguish nervousness from defiance, but a defendant who disrupts orderly proceedings must be constrained. If there is undue interruption, it is often best to put the represented defendant, in the first instance, into the hands of his advocate. If this fails, the chairman will have to warn and, if unheeded, act by having him removed from the court.

An unrepresented defendant may need careful handling by the chairman. However, the court is not required to exercise endless patience. The vexatious defendant has to be controlled. The angry defendant should be admonished firmly, courteously and briefly, and, if necessary, warned of the ultimate sanction of his removal from court. Equally, an unduly reticent defendant should be encouraged to give all the evidence which is relevant to the case. A phrase such as 'Take your time and tell us in your own words what happened' may be helpful.

Behaviour counts more than dress, in the dock or in the witness box. Non-comforming attire can be tolerated there which would be unacceptable on the bench or on others.

The chairman should ensure that the defendant has an opportunity to exercise his rights. He must see that the unrepresented have an opportunity to consult a solicitor or apply for legal aid. A refusal of bail should be accompanied by information as to the right to apply for bail to the High Court or the Crown Court (see chapter 5 under head (1), Bail). If the defendant persists in being unrepresented and pleads guilty, the court must take particular care that he understands the charge and admits the offence. A plea of not guilty should be substituted for one of guilty if it becomes clear at any point in the proceedings that the plea is equivocal. The defendant may say that he wants 'to get it over with', or indicate he has not understood that what he regarded as morally wrong may not, in law, amount to an offence. 'I forgot to pay' is a potential defence to theft from a shop. If a defendant casts doubt on his guilty plea during mitigation and the court has seen his record, his case will have to be heard by another bench.

At all times the defendant should be seen to have the full attention of the court. If the chairman has to sign documents, he would be well advised to halt proceedings until he has done so. Proper provision should be made for every recess. The chairman should allow reasonable time for the police to organise the defendants' meals and to have their own. He should also, without having to be prompted, extend bail where applicable.

INTERPRETERS

Interpreters are vital to just decision in any case in which there could be some doubt as to the defendant's understanding of proceedings. Chairman will want to accommodate them as conveniently near the defendants as possible and to check that they can keep pace.

With witnesses

Witnesses are members of the public. They are rendering a public service. The chairman will be aware that this often involves personal strain and inconvenience.

In a system which places so much weight on oral evidence, much depends on the credibility of witnesses. The chairman should make sure that all can hear what the witness says. He should observe the witness carefully. Honest witnesses may be inhibited by the unfamiliar proceedings or the courtroom. A skilful but dishonest witness can impress. Equally, inaccurate evidence may be due to selective perception rather than dishonesty. The confident and articulate are not necessarily more reliable than the diffident and tongue-tied. A good way to test the reliability of a witness is to note the consistency of what he says and his steadfastness under cross-examination.

There are hazards for the honest witness. They include bias, often unconscious, in favour of a friend, of an accomplice or of the victim; and the vagaries of memory. Memory can be refreshed from a written note. There are certain conditions of which the bench must be aware before allowing a witness to refresh his memory from a written note. It must have been made by the witness, or read over by him, and he must accept it as accurate. It must have been written when the facts were still fresh in his memory. Fresh is difficult to define. One month and three months have been judged too long. Surprisingly, an interval of twenty-two days has been accepted.[5]

5 *Stone's Justices' Manual* (1987), para 2-33.

Corroborative evidence is clearly desirable, even when not required by law. It is necessary when the witness is a child too young to take the oath.

It is good practice for witnesses to remain out of court until called. The chairman should make sure that this practice is followed. At the conclusion of their testimony, witnesses should be thanked for their services (but not for their evidence). They may be released on request and with the agreement of the parties. It used to be the practice for witnesses who had given evidence to sit at the back of the court until the case was finished. This practice ensured they did not talk to others still to be called. This fail-safe against influencing other witnesses has advantages. The chairman should tell those who have given evidence to sit at the back of the court. There may occasionally be grounds for commending a witness at the very end of the proceedings. Courage, or outstanding public spirit, could well be acknowledged, but sparingly. To punctuate the proceedings with praise would give an unfortunate impression of bias towards a particular testimony. Commendation should never be given in a case being committed to the Crown Court for trial.

In questioning a witness on his own or his colleagues' behalf, a chairman should ensure that his questions are elucidatory and do not break fresh ground. If the prosecuting solicitor fails to bring evidence on a material point, this may mean that the case is not proved. The omission should not be rectified by the chairman. Nevertheless, when an obvious point seems to be in danger of being overlooked, a question such as 'Are we going to hear evidence as to the state of the road?' is in order. Chairmen should not inhibit the flow of a line of questioning, but sometimes a choice has to be made between interrupting at the time to clear up a slight ambiguity or waiting until the end of the evidence. Clarification at once may make what follows more intelligible. Questions left until the end have the advantage that they will follow those of the opposing advocate, who may well have anticipated them. Evidence is often in chronologically muddled sequence, and this needs to be patiently sorted out by questions from the bench. Sequence can be pertinent to decision.

Expert witnesses present less difficulty. They have special knowledge and no stake in the issue. The chairman's questions should ensure that what has been stated in a specialist field is clearly understood on the bench.

Victims appear most frequently as witnesses. The National Association of Victim Support Schemes has underlined the vital contribution of the victim to the detection of crime and the just disposal of the criminal. It increasingly ensures support for the victim prior to and following the court hearing. But the way in which victims and witnesses are treated in court is a matter for the chairman. A report, 'Witnesses in Court', published by Justice, claims that they are often treated with indifference or discourtesy, given little notice of the trial, summoned brusquely, and kept hanging around outside the courtroom. In court they are made to stand, may be questioned in a hostile manner, are not thanked, or told what to do next. Victims are often not informed as to the outcome of the case.

Chairmen may feel it appropriate to discuss these issues at a bench meeting. They might deal with the reception of witnesses and, where premises permit, with separate waiting facilities so that prosecution and defence witnesses do not mingle. The question of when witnesses might be offered the option of giving evidence seated could also be considered. An explanatory leaflet covering these and other matters could be invaluable.

The chairman personally will only encounter the victim as a witness. He should treat him with customary courtesy and consideration but can show no partiality towards him.

With the police

Police witnesses have no privileged status. Neither should they have in magistrates' minds. In the case of *R v Bingham Justices, ex p Jowitt*[6] a conviction was quashed because the chairman had said:

> Quite the most unpleasant cases that we have to decide are those where the evidence is a direct conflict between a police officer and a member of the public. My principle in such cases has always been to believe the evidence of the police officer, and therefore we find the case proved.

Nevertheless, the police are not lay witnesses in uniform. They are trained and experienced observers, taught how to give evidence and subject to a code of discipline.

Police in the witness box frequently ask to refresh their memories from their notebooks. If, on enquiry by the chairman, there is no objection from the parties and the notes are contemporaneous with the incident, they should be permitted to do so.

Police are usually the jailers in court. Magistrates often recoil from their having placed handcuffs on the defendant. The chairman should recognise that the police are responsible for security and must have a discretion in this matter.

With the probation officer

Justices aim to select the disposal which will reduce the risk of re-

6 (1974) Times, 3 July.

offending or recidivism. Here they often depend on the probation service for information, assessment and recommendation. For many offenders the price of liberty is involvement with the probation service. This may be true after conviction, whether in or out of custody. Probation officers work in prison to see a man through his incarceration, to assist him to regain his freedom by remission or parole and, by his after care, to ensure that liberty regained is liberty retained.

Chairmen need to understand the approach of the probation officer to whom a defendant is a client or potential client. The probation service is not merely a social service but part of the criminal justice system of the country along with the courts, the police, and the custodial and non-custodial institutions. A probation officer's loyalty may therefore be divided and the bench should be sensitive to his difficulties when assessing the weight to attach to any recommendation he may make for the judicial disposal of the accused.

There can be no doubt that probation officers serve the court. A chairman may be concerned about the time they sit and wait. This waiting time has increased with the advent of legal aid and duty solicitors, who have taken on some jobs previously done by probation officers. A chairman, having consulted his colleagues, can put a case back for a probation officer (in the absence of a duty solicitor) to help a defendant understand the proceedings or to grasp why an equivocal plea of guilty cannot be accepted 'just to get it over with'. A discussion between a probation officer and a defendant may result in a realistic offer of a rate of payment of a financial penalty. A short adjournment may enable a probation officer to find out if a 'stand down' report, which obviates the need for a further remand for a full social inquiry report and the cost and inconvenience of re-convening the court, would meet the needs of the case.

Probation reports are provided to the court and should not be shown or distributed to anybody, including the advocates, without its authority. The chairman should protect the confidentiality of the report. This is not always appreciated by advocates who may view early access to the report as a useful adjunct to mitigation. There is no bar to their having sight of a report before coming into court provided this is with the knowledge and acquiescence of the bench. Early disclosure enables advocates to take instructions and reduce delay. It may be fairer. The chairman must see to it in court that a copy of the social inquiry report is given to the offender.[7]

7 Powers of Criminal Courts Act 1973, s 46(1).

Provided a probation officer is on the premises and available to each court, it should not be expected that he will be present at every sitting. The author of a particular report may not be able to attend the hearing of the case. Then it is vital that the probation officer on court duty is fully briefed as to the background of the report. Probation reports may lose some standing if there is no one in court who can answer questions arising from them. As much of the report will be hearsay evidence, the appropriate oath is the *voire dire*.[8] Any dialogue with the chairman which might give the impression that the probation officer is taking part in sentencing should be avoided.

The defence lawyer may call his client to give evidence concerning the report. This sometimes corrects or sharpens the focus. If the chairman thinks that such a course would be helpful, he should invite the lawyer to call his client. It is imperative that courts make no decision with the wool, however, unintentionally, pulled over their eyes.

With the public

Currently, law and order seem to be increasingly challenged and courts can occasionally become targets of less than orderly behaviour. Lord Hailsham was alive to the danger when, in addressing the joint Conference of the Cumberland, Westmoreland and Furness Branch of the Magistrates' Association in April 1973, he said:

> Do not allow your court to be made into a bear garden or a forum for political demonstration, never hesitate if need arises to direct the police to clear the gallery or the well of the court or to remove the individual demonstrator if he makes a disturbance. Court hearings are to be heard in silence. The right of the public is to listen, not participate.[9]

The chairman's function can escalate from prevention, through intervention, to decisive action. His aim is prevention. Good equipment for the preventive role is court awareness: being alive to the total situation in the courtroom while keeping the central proceedings in sharp focus.

Often by a look or word a chairman forestalls a potential disruption. A warning shot across the bows may be all that is necessary if it is absolutely clear that further violation will be followed by action.

8 The *voire dire:* 'I swear by Almighty God that I will true answer make to all such questions as the court shall demand of me.'
9 (1973) 29 The Magistrate at p 101.

When decisive action becomes necessary, the chairman will not hesitate. If an individual is at fault, he may deal with him himself. If there is more general disorder from the public, the wisest course may be for the bench to withdraw to allow the police to deal with the situation. There are statutory procedures, detailed below, for dealing with contempt. A chairman needs to have these at his finger tips.

CONTEMPT OF COURT

Section 12 of the Contempt of Court Act 1981 provides that:

> Where any person wilfully insults the justice or justices, any witness before or officer of the court or any solicitor or counsel having business in the court, during his or their sitting or attendance in court, or in going to or returning from the court, or wilfully interrupts the proceedings of the court or otherwise misbehaves in court, the court may order any officer of the court or any constable to take the offender into custody and detain him until the rising of the court: and the court may, if it thinks fit, commit the offender to custody for a specified period not exceeding one month or impose on him a fine not exceeding £1,000 or both.

These powers are expressed in very wide terms. It is perhaps surprising that magistrates possessed no statutory or other clearly stated powers to deal with contempt until 1981. However, an adjournment to let things cool down, or, in more serious instances, a binding over with or without sureties, usually dealt with disturbances. So there was no great pressure from magistrates themselves for a new power to deal with contempt. Section 12 nevertheless provides a most useful additional remedy. It empowers magistrates to deal with conduct which clearly interferes with the administration of justice. It extends the justices' powers to protect a witness, a solicitor or counsel 'in going to or returning from the court'.

We would offer a word of caution about the use of the power to commit to custody in section 12. It should be exercised with restraint, and only when it is clear that no lesser step will suffice. Any contempt is of course a serious matter if it strikes at the roots of justice, but a chairman should not take the insult personally. The contempt is of the court. An opportunity must be given for an apology. If that is not immediately forthcoming, detention until the rising of the court will, in many cases, be sufficient to induce a change of mind and attitude. If a committal to custody is made, a magistrates' court may at any time revoke it and order the offender's discharge.

Disturbers of the peace are frequently peripatetic. The way in which one court deals with contempt may therefore have repercussions for others in a reduction of challenges to good order elsewhere.

TAPE RECORDERS

Another useful provision of the Contempt of Court Act 1981 is in section 9. It provides that it is a contempt of court to use in court, or bring into court for use, any tape recorder or other instrument for recording sound, without the leave of the court. It is also contempt of court to publish a recording of legal proceedings or to use any such recording in contravention of any conditions which the court may have attached to the grant of permission to use the equipment in court. The discretion in the court to grant, withhold or withdraw leave is unlimited but a *Practice Direction*[10] lists the following factors as relevant to its exercise:

(a) the existence of any reasonable need on the part of the applicant for leave, whether a litigant or a person connected with the press or broadcasting, for the record to be made;
(b) in a criminal case, or in a civil case in which a direction has been given excluding one or more witnesses from the court, the risk that the recording may be used for the purpose of briefing witnesses out of court;
(c) any possibility that the use of a recorder would disturb the proceedings or distract or worry any witness or other participants.

THE PRESS

If the court is cleared because of disorder, the press can remain as representatives of the public. Justice is still not only to be done, but is to be seen to be done.

Reporting is vital to a democracy. Lord Hailsham, in addressing the Annual General Meeting of the Magistrates' Association in 1971, said of the press: 'What goes on in court is public property and it is not merely their right but their duty to report and very often their duty to comment. Private justice is almost always a denial of justice'.[11]

The cloak of anonymity should not shroud the chairman, or for that matter his colleagues. In July 1985 the Council of the Magistrates' Association passed a resolution in the following terms:

> It does not appear necessary, and will frequently be impracticable, for the names of adjudicating magistrates to be publicly listed before courts sit.

10 [1981] 3 All ER 848.
11 (1973) 29 The Magistrate at p 50.

> The names of adjudicating magistrates should normally be available on request by persons having a bona fide interest (eg prosecutor or defendant or their legal representatives or press representatives) during or after proceedings in court but there will be a small number of occasions when it will be in the interest of justice for the names to be withheld.
>
> Names should be withheld where there are substantial grounds for belief that the magistrates concerned, or members of their families, or other associates, might, in consequence of the proceedings, be subject to violence or harassment. Examples are where defendants are members of terrorist groups, or of other organisations habitually using violence or harassment to achieve or publicise their objectives.

In *R v Felixstowe Justices, ex p Leigh*[12], decided in October 1986, Lord Justice Watkins stated that there was, in his view, no such person known to law as the anonymous JP. The applicants in this case, the proprietors of The Observer and Mr David Leigh, a journalist, sought (1) an order of mandamus directing the Clerk to the Felixstowe Justices to disclose to Mr Leigh the names of the justices sitting in a particular case, and (2) a declaration that the policy of the Justices and the Clerk as a matter of discretion or otherwise to withhold from the public and the press the identity of justices either hearing or who have heard cases, was contrary to law. The declaration sought was granted, but mandamus was refused. It was held that Mr Leigh did not have sufficient interest in the disclosure of the justices' names as his aim was not to report the case but to comment on the various issues arising out of the report of the case by others.

The basis of the case is the 'open justice' principle. It was held that a policy such as that maintained by the Felixstowe Justices and their Clerk was inimical to the proper administration of justice and an unwarranted and unlawful obstruction to the right to know who sits in judgment. A bona fide enquirer is entitled to know the name of a justice who is sitting or who has sat on a case recently heard.

It is clear that the right to know relates to the name of a justice. No one can demand his address or telephone number.

The case was concerned with the public's right to know the names of justices adjudicating. Questions about anonymity occasionally arise in a wider context. It is interesting that a letter from the Secretary of Commissions to the National Council of Civil Liberties was quoted in the case. It was written on 24 February 1981, on behalf of the Lord Chancellor, and expresses a wider principle. Part of it is in these terms:

12 [1987] 2 WLR 380.

There is no statutory provision either prohibiting or requiring the publication of the names of Justices of the Peace. A general list of local justices is normally available at any courthouse, and the only reason why the identity of justices in a particular area might not be revealed to a person or organisation would normally be the risk that the information was required in order to facilitate harassment, intimidation or other threats or dangers to the magistrates concerned. Such a problem sometimes arises in a particular case, where a dissatisfied litigant seeks personal retribution against the Bench concerned. In short, therefore, any person or body should be entitled to know the identity of the local magistracy, unless there is some manifest reason in the public interest to refuse it in the particular case.

In the *Felixstowe Justices* case Lord Justice Watkins said that a clerk to the justices would be justified in refusing, during or after a hearing, to give the name of one of the justices to a person who the clerk reasonably believes requires that information solely for an improper purpose.

With colleagues

The good reason why, at any rate on not guilty pleas, three magistrates are regarded as an ideal number to constitute a bench is that there is safety for the defendant in the checks and balances of discussion among this number. This discussion may be one explanation of the low number of appeals from magistrates' courts. Three is a manageable number for consultation in court. Moreover, it gives scope for each member to contribute to a discussion in depth in the retiring room. It makes a majority decision – though it must never be disclosed as such – more attainable.

Questions to witnesses are put through the chair. It may be neater if the chairman tells his colleagues whether he prefers them whispered to him or written down. The chairman will not veto a question which a colleague regards as necessary to his own decision making. He needs to ensure, however, that the question does not offend the rules of evidence or amount to mere repetition, or is otherwise improper. Sometimes a colleague with special knowledge may wish to put a technical question. Here the chairman may well invite him to put it himself. When there are minor matters which need to be corrected or clarified, such as a date, it is often preferable for the chairman to intervene immediately, during the giving of the evidence. Constant interruptions are to be avoided, however, since they deflect a train of thought or the flow of argument to the detriment of the case which is being put.

Consultation with colleagues on any matter concerning the defendant or witnesses, as distinct from the management of the court, should be manifest. Colleagues should be consulted about whether to retire to their room to give a matter consideration. Observers will draw conclusions from the disappearances and re-appearances of the bench. If the magistrates do not retire, they can give the impression of scant consideration of a case despite the fact that they have been giving it deep thought from the moment it opened. Conversely, a restless bench, constantly retiring on minor issues, may seem to have difficulty in making up its mind. The bench should always act as necessary to decision. An experienced bench is unlikely to need to retire as frequently as an inexperienced one. Any request from one of its number to retire should be granted, particularly if there is disagreement on the bench or the case is complex or involves several defendants.

There is High Court guidance on the importance of being seen to consult in court in *R v Newly*.[13] It was claimed that a recorder had not consulted the two magistrates sitting with him before announcing a prison sentence. The Court of Appeal accepted that they had conferred prior to court, and passed notes during the speech in mitigation. Nevertheless, it emphasises the need to be seen to consult.

A court represents a dynamic situation. The participants mentioned in this chapter are independent and yet interdependent. An astute chairman regulates their interaction and ensures, within the confines of prescribed procedure, that the court's dispensation of justice is efficient, unruffled and fair.

13 *R v Newly* (1984) Crim LR 509.

Chapter 3

The relationship with the clerk

HISTORY

Over the last forty years subtle changes have taken place in the relationship between magistrates and their clerk. Improvements in the training of magistrates have made them less reliant on him. Even more fundamental has been the change in the role of the clerk. We have seen the part-time clerk give way to his full-time counterpart and simultaneously we have seen the amalgamation of petty sessional divisions. The background to all these changes has been a massive increase in the volume of business. The clerk to the justices is at the head of a complex administrative machine. He is responsible for the smooth running of all aspects of the court as well as being legal adviser to the justices.

The pressure of administrative responsibilities has meant that many justices' clerks go into court only infrequently, and some not at all. So, whereas in the past a chairman would have the familiar back of the neck of the clerk to the justices or his deputy in front of him he will now find in all probability that he has a court clerk assistant below him. In London, and some other places, it would be the side of his face as the clerk sits at right angles to the bench rather than with his back to the bench, as is traditional in other parts of the country.

The bench/clerk relationship, and more specifically the chairman/clerk relationship, is a cornerstone of our system of summary justice. Many critics of the system overlook the crucial role that clerks play, and thus miss the essence of the matter. The system is most at risk when the relationship is not working well. The *East Kerrier* case decided in 1952[1] and the *Practice Direction*[2] which

1 *R v East Kerrier Justices, ex p Mundy* [1952] 2 All ER 144. See Sir Thomas Skyrme *The Changing Image of the Magistracy*. pp 180-183 (second edn).

2 [1953] 2 All ER 1306.

followed were probably the result of a feeling at the time that some clerks were too dominant and needed to have their wings clipped. Like many impressions, this feeling, if it was ever justified, lingered on long after it had ceased to be generally true.

In 1974 the Magistrates' Association and the Justices' Clerks Society produced a summary of existing law and good practice entitled *The Lay Justices and the Clerk in the Magistrates' Court.* Although a little dated, as regards the chairman's role, it is still of value and is reproduced here at appendix I. In 1981 a further *Practice Direction*[3] emphasised the nature of the relationship. It is worthy of study in detail and is reproduced here at appendix II. Now, in *R v Uxbridge Justices, ex p Smith*[4] the spectre of *East Kerrier* seems finally to have been laid to rest, as it is established that the clerk may enter the retiring room uninvited, in appropriate circumstances.

In that, a drink/driving case, the court clerk concerned asked the defendant's counsel for the references to passages he had quoted from *Wilkinson's Road Traffic Offences.* When she had looked these up she formed the view that the submissions were wrong in law. Having told counsel what she proposed to do, she left the courtroom and went to the retiring room. She returned to court some twenty minutes later. Shortly afterwards the justices returned and announced that they found the case proved. It was argued on appeal that the clerk should not have left the court to advise the justices uninvited and that her advice should have been tendered in open court. These arguments were not accepted.

It would probably be wise in circumstances such as these for the clerk to invite the justices to return to court so that advice could be given. However, there are times when it would not be improper for the justices to receive confidential advice from their clerk. It is heartening that the case emphasised the confidential nature of the relationship between magistrates and clerks in contrast to the somewhat negative *East Kerrier* approach to that relationship. Of course appearances are important. Justice must be seen to be done. It must be clear that the decision is that of the justices. Even in the *Uxbridge* case the Divisional Court made it plain that they would interfere in any case where it seemed that the clerk had played an improper role. For the sake of completeness, the statutory provisions in the Justices of the Peace Act 1979, section 28(3) and (4) as to the functions of a clerk are set out in appendix III.

3 [1981] 2 All ER 831.
4 (1985) Times, 6 May.

COMPLEMENTARY ROLES

The chairman and clerk have quite separate but complementary roles. It is true that justices are judges both of fact and law, but as a matter of good practice justices should accept the clerk's advice on matters of law, practice and procedure (appendix I, paragraph 6). There are matters which are justices' territory and there are matters which are clerks' territory. The chairman and the clerk should be scrupulous about this. Verdict and sentence are for the justices. Law, practice and procedure are for the clerk. The distinction is not always clear. An experienced chairman will have sufficient confidence to handle those matters which are in the grey area, himself. This is all to the good as it creates a favourable public impression of the competence of the court. However, a wise chairman will be aware of his limitations. Equally, he should have sufficient working knowledge of practice and procedure to be seen to be in control.

If the clerk appears to be in control, it is the chairman's fault. An over-assertive clerk, and happily there are few these days, should be checked, tactfully of course, but firmly. A chairman who is hesitant or unsure of himself will create a situation in which a clerk may be forced to intervene in order to keep proceedings on the rails. A wise chairman who is unsure on any point will not let the situation drift but will ask the clerk. An experienced clerk will assist a new chairman and give advice in a manner which does not embarrass the bench or undermine the dignity of the court's proceedings. Equally, all court clerks have to learn. Occasionally a chairman may find himself with a clerk who is inexperienced. Nothing is more demoralising for a young 'learner' clerk than public exposure of any gaucherie, so a chairman needs to handle this with sensitivity.

It is in relation to the court clerk that the 1981 *Practice Direction* gives some of its most specific guidance about the role of the justices' clerk. It makes clear that the justices' clerk himself is responsible for the way in which his assistants advise the justices 'even when he is not sitting with the justices as clerk of the court'. The pattern in many larger courts these days is for the justices' clerk to remain in his office and for the courts to be manned by his assistants. He will be available to advise any justice or clerk. Chairmen should not be slow to ask for the justices' clerk's personal advice. This may pose problems if a court is held at a courthouse some distance away from the justices' clerk's office. These problems should not be insuperable. They are never a reason, in themselves, not to seek guidance. Some arrangements should exist for the tendering of advice in all circumstances.

In the past it was common for the least experienced chairman to sit with the least experienced clerk, an arrangement which has been increasingly recognised as undesirable. Many benches now take steps to ensure that there is a blend of experience. Monitoring the performance of chairmen and clerks is not always easy. Colleagues of chairmen have a method of expressing their views at the annual elections; a justices' clerk rarely has the opportunity to observe his staff in court. To be called in by the chairman or court clerk to advise is a valuable chance for him to see how his assistant is measuring up.

Some courts may be more difficult to preside over than others but there is no such thing as an easy court. A chairman and clerk must always be prepared to deal with the unexpected. 'Simple' traffic cases have a nasty habit of producing the most complex issues of law – or an awkward defendant! It is never a sign of weakness for a chairman to recognise he does not know what to do; rather the reverse. If in doubt, 'ask the clerk' must be the cardinal rule.

Not that the clerk always has to wait to be asked for advice. If he is aware of any point of law, practice or procedure which he feels is material, he may of his own initiative bring this to the court's attention. This is so even if the justices have already retired to consider their decision, although it is probably better to invite them to return to court so that the advice can be tendered in public. This is certainly the wiser course if the clerk wishes to offer advice on any matter which has not been previously argued in the case by the advocates, so that they can have an opportunity of commenting on the advice tendered. However, it is established that justices are entitled to confidential advice from their clerk, so while it may be a desirable practice that as much advice as possible should be tendered in open court, and that whispered conversations between clerk and justices should be kept to a minimum, there will always be occasions when a whispered conversation or advice in the privacy of the retiring room is appropriate.

OUT OF THE ARENA

It is a not uncommon experience for justices to feel that everyone in court is conspiring to keep from them some vital information in a case. Sometimes this is unavoidable. The evidence may be inadmissible for some reason. It is as well for a chairman to have this basic point in mind when he is contemplating introducing some new line of questioning. If the parties are represented, this should not generally be attempted. It must be annoying to an advocate if, working carefully up to a question in cross-examination, he finds that it is suddenly asked by the court. Neither the chairman nor the clerk should enter into the dust of the arena. The clerk may properly assist an unrepresented defendant in the conduct of his case but even this task should be approached with some care.

The division of functions between chairman and clerk is important. Administrative matters should be left to the clerk. Decisions of the bench should be announced by the chairman. Matters relating to public order or the decorum of the court should generally be dealt with by the chairman. In the middle ground there is room for personal inclination. In some courts the chairman administers the oath to witnesses (though this is not a practice generally approved); in others it is the clerk's or the usher's duty. Should it be the chairman or clerk who puts questions to the defendant during a means enquiry? Here the practice varies. Whatever the division of duties, it is essential that the chairman and clerk come to some understanding on the matter. The worst result of all is silence, while each waits for the other.

A crucial part of the relationship is the preparation for arriving at decisions as to whether or not the case is proved and what sentence or order is to follow. We deal with this separately (p 33). By way of introduction, we include here some comments on the taking of notes of evidence.

The 1981 *Practice Direction* gives some guidance in paragraph 4, appendix II. It is entirely a matter for justices to decide for themselves whether they will take notes of the evidence and, if they do, how full they are. Traditionally clerks have taken a fairly full note of the evidence and in some courts the clerk may have an assistant present to take a full note. With the vast increase in work in recent years, there has been a tendency for some clerks to take only minimal notes or none at all. Clerks who adopt this practice rely on the absence of statutory obligation for them to take a note of the evidence on a summary trial. It may be difficult for a clerk to fulfil his responsibility to his justices to refresh their memory as to the evidence if he keeps no note at all. It would be sensible for chairman and clerk to decide how a sufficient note is to be taken. Paragraph 4(c) of the *Practice Direction* is worthy of particular attention. It states that if justices wish to consult their clerk solely about the evidence or his notes of it, they shall ordinarily, and certainly in simple cases, do so in open court. The object of the *Practice Direction* is to avoid any suspicion that the clerk has been involved in decisions on issues of fact. It also presupposes that the clerk has a note.

A competent chairman and a competent clerk working

harmoniously together make court proceedings run smoothly. Even the most disjointed list or trying circumstance will not loosen their joint grasp on proceedings. They will present a formidable united front to the most difficult party or advocate, and together will be able sensitively to guide the most diffident and nervous witness through his trying experience in the witness box.

Chapter 4

The retiring room

The retiring room has two different functions: judicial and social. Before and after court hearings, it is a place for social interchange. This may be somewhat more circumscribed preparatory to the day's hearing, more relaxed at the end. When justices retire during judicial deliberations, the room is private to a particular bench. No one enters except the clerk of the court or the clerk to the justices if further advice is needed. Both come usually by invitation.

THE RETIRING ROOM PRIOR TO COURT

The judicial day begins in the retiring room. Here the chairman can get to know his bench colleagues. Recently appointed magistrates can be welcomed and incorporated. It can be a sorting office for queries great and small. Some of these arise when justices are allocated to the various courts. Methods of allocation vary. If they work, there is no reason for change. What follows has been found suitable in some courts.

The clerk puts up a preliminary list allocating justices to specific courts. The chairman looks at this to ensure that the inexperienced sit with the experienced and that those prevented from sitting in their allotted court, by acquaintance, friendship or relationship with particular defendants, witnesses or advocates, are moved to an alternative court or don't sit at all. Whether or not a magistrate is so barred depends on a number of factors. He may make his own decision to withdraw for reasons of conscience or partiality. It is imperative that on examination of the composition of the bench, justice is seen to be done.

Early training will have acquainted a justice with statutory disqualifications. He is debarred if he is personally interested in the outcome of a case, for example if it relates to damage to his property or an assault on his daughter. In marginal cases the decision as to whether an individual is disqualified causes more difficulty. The chairman will probably have to decide. When, for instance, the justice is an executive in a large company and the defendant his employee, even if he has no personal acquaintance with him, the hearing should start with a disclosure of the fact and the parties be invited to accept or reject his jurisdiction. A disqualifying factor may arise unexpectedly in court. If, during the proceedings, a justice recognises a defendant or witness with whom he is in a relationship which might debar him from sitting, he should leave the bench for a position in the courtroom, where it is apparent he can take no further part in that case. The chairman's role is to announce that his colleague is no longer adjudicating. Such a justice must not withdraw to the retiring room to which the adjudicating justices may later adjourn to deliberate.

Magistrates may be called from the retiring room prior to the day's hearings when, for example, warrants or summonses are requested or police officers are to be sworn. The chairman may encourage a justice who needs a little more confidence or experience to undertake these tasks. He may, alternatively, prefer to give a recently appointed justice the opportunity of watching an experienced one at work. The decision is often taken informally. One is wary of rejecting volunteers. However, competence is important and should weigh in the chairman's decision. Inefficiency from the bench does little to enhance public regard for magistrates.

THE RETIRING ROOM DURING A HEARING

During proceedings, retirement has any but its normal meaning. The chairman is responsible for getting the deliberations started. They should last as long as is necessary to consider fully the evidence and not a minute more. In court, defendants are in suspense and sometimes their families even more so. Time is money. This is especially important because of legal aid. Delay in court is partly the cumulative effect of cases on which justices have spent more time in the retiring room than necessary.

Preventing unnecessary delay is a matter for the chairman. True, he has no casting vote and his status is that accorded to him by his colleagues. Nevertheless, it is he who structures the discussions. A chairman may find that an analysis of the processes and sequence of decision making (see appendix IV) will help him to guide rather than lead deliberations. Verdict and sentence are a total response to a complex situation. Not every step in the sequence from evidence to decision will always be taken overtly. Much depends on the experience of the bench and the complexity of the situation. Some colleagues reach a decision taking several steps at a time. Others require a lengthy discussion. The speed of decision-making has to be the speed of the slowest member, to ensure maximum participation. The chairman is there to see that no undue pressure is exercised.

Deliberations in the retiring room provide a good training opportunity for the chairman. A structured discussion is confined to the evidence, and avoids waste of time. There can be no straying along non-judicial by-ways. Training should have eliminated the attitude 'I always believe the police when it is their word against anybody else's'. Similarly, training should have increased magistrates' comprehension of their sentencing powers. The chairman should not have to correct 'I don't think he should go to prison, I think he should have a suspended sentence'.

Perhaps the most tedious and time wasting of all is the colleague who does not so much try a particular offence as a whole way of life. He can be censorious to a degree and deplore conduct he does not understand embarked on under pressures he has never experienced. He is slow to learn that self-indulgent moralising offers no escape from the solemn duty of administering justice. The morally and legally wrong do not always coincide. Magistrates are on the bench solely to deal with particular offences presented in court according to the rules of evidence. Prejudice, suspicion and supposition have no more place in the retiring room than they have in court. It is part of the chairman's task to ensure that they do not emerge there.

The chairman should give each colleague an equal chance to speak and equal attentiveness. He should be aware of their strengths and weaknesses and be ready to use any special knowledge likely to be illuminating, for instance the credibility to be attached to financial statements as to wages and benefits. An expert, however, may himself need guidance. Following an account of injuries, for example, a doctor may have to recognise that he can use his expertise in deciding the weight which can be put on the evidence, but he will have to draw the line at giving what amounts to expert evidence to his colleagues in the retiring room, in contradiction to or in addition to what they have heard in court. There is a High Court direction for the justice who is a specialist in any particular field.[1] It makes clear that he can apply his basic

1 *Weatherall v Harrison* [1976] 1 All ER 241.

knowledge in assessing evidence before the court. He would be well advised to wait until he is asked. Then he could reveal the way in which his specialist knowledge accords with the evidence, though he should never unduly press his views on his colleagues. No evidence should be given behind the closed doors of the retiring room.

When decisions are being reached, chairmen follow different schools of thought as to whether to disclose their own view first or last. We advocate that the most recently appointed magistrate should contribute first. On a bench of the optimum size of three, this saves him the potential embarrassment of having a casting vote. More importantly, it underlines the obligation of each justice to know and to speak his own independent mind. His first view is not necessarily immutable. A justice will discover that to change his mind for sound and stated reasons gains nothing but respect and understanding from colleagues. All of us, at one time or another, have owed a debt of gratitude to colleagues who have caused us to change our minds because of their greater knowledge, superior wisdom or deeper insight.

A unanimous decision is preferable but not attained invariably. A magistrate is sometimes concerned that, having dissented from a verdict, he is required to assist in sentencing. Here the chairman will be alert to any consequential attempt to mitigate sentence. There is a parallel in that statute allows one court to sentence following a finding of guilt by another.

The confidentiality of the retiring room is sacrosanct. A chairman should be satisfied that his colleagues appreciate the need for non-disclosure. There can be no disclosure of the process of decision-making, or of whether it was unanimous or of the discussion on verdict or sentence. Social conversation should never go beyond what could have been learned by those present in court at the hearing.

THE CLERK IN THE RETIRING ROOM

It is the responsibility of the clerk to the justices, or the court clerk to whom he delegates it, to advise on questions of law or mixed law and fact and on practice and procedure. This he can do on his own initiative. Justices may not be aware, for instance, of judicial decisions which are binding on them. They may not have read relevant circulars from the Home Office. More frequently, the clerk advises them on request. One of the most important qualifications of the chairman is to realise when to ask. In the retiring room he is usually the spokesman for his colleagues to the clerk. It would be improper to seek the clerk's advice on guilt or innocence so far as this is a question of fact. The clerk must play no part in the decision on that. It is important that the procedure adopted by the justices when they retire makes this abundantly clear.

The clerk should never retire with them as a matter of course. When it is appropriate for him to retire with the justices, for example where it is obvious that an issue of law has been raised, the chairman should announce that the justices are asking their clerk to retire with them to advise them on the law.

As we have already noted (p 24), circumstances can arise which make it appropriate for the clerk to enter the retiring room uninvited.[2] He should stay only as long as is necessary for him to give the advice required. Otherwise the impression can be created that he has become another member of the bench. As a matter of general practice, the clerk should return to court before the justices to avoid this difficulty.

It is not improper for the clerk to remain with the magistrates for substantially the whole of their adjournment if this is justified by the circumstances. Where questions of fact and law are closely interwoven, it may be necessary for the clerk to be present to hear the discussion between the justices so that he can advise them on the law. In the Crown Court, counsel for the prosecution and defence normally draw attention to relevant matters of law. Furthermore, in the Crown Court the judge will sum up for the jury so that they will retire with the issues to be decided clearly in mind. Magistrates are unlikely to have the benefit of such a clear exposition of the legal issues. It is proper for the clerk to advise in open court, and this practice is to be encouraged. It enables the public and parties to hear the advice tendered, and gives an advocate an opportunity to comment on the advice.

In a complicated case, magistrates may wish the clerk to go over the main issues to be decided, in the retiring room, whether or not he has already given assistance on this in open court. In some cases, it may assist if justices indicate their findings of fact to the clerk, as it will enable his advice to be much more specific. The need for advice is most likely to arise in a case in which there is a direct conflict of evidence on the facts, so that the issues of law are different depending upon which version of events is believed.

To take a simple example involving only two witnesses, the police officer and the defendant on a charge of carrying an offensive weapon. The police officer gives evidence that he saw the defendant brandishing a stick during a fight between youths outside the local

2 *R v Uxbridge Magistrates' Court, ex p Smith* (1985) 149 JP 620.

discotheque, and that when he questioned him about his possession of the stick the defendant said that he had taken it with him that night because he thought there might be trouble with a gang from a neighbouring town. The defendant denies this and says in evidence on oath that he picked the stick up in the heat of the moment after the fight had broken out. He admits in cross-examination that he would have used the stick if attacked. In re-examination he says that what he means is that he would have used it in self defence as the other youths were considerably bigger than he was. Several points of law arise here; principally whether the defendant 'had with him' an offensive weapon.

It would be possible for the clerk to give a general review of the law on the matter before the justices retire, but the advice will be much more to the point if the justices say to the clerk, 'We find that the defendant picked up the stick in the heat of the moment after the fight commenced, but that he would have used it offensively. What is the law on the matter?'

If the clerk is not present when a complicated case is being discussed, he will have no opportunity of pointing out any misunderstanding on law, practice and procedure on the part of the bench, in arriving at their decision. Although the clerk must take no part in deciding sentence, it is appropriate for him to advise on such matters as the intention of Parliament through legislation, on the statutory maximum penalty and the level of sentence imposed by their own and other benches for the type of offence under consideration.

If a bench is uneasy about the advice given, perhaps when a court clerk is himself relatively inexperienced or coming upon a problem for the first time, the chairman should seek the advice of the clerk to the justices.

It is a wise preparation for the chairman to inform the clerk of the court of the proposed sentence before he announces it. The clerk can confirm its legality and note it down. This assists him, particularly when there are multiple offences or offenders. This practice also eliminates the need for consultation between bench and clerk during the announcement, which diminishes the dignity of the court at a critical stage in its proceedings.

It is in the retiring room that the collective function of the bench is most fully experienced. Within its walls, generations of chairmen have shared responsibility for the administration of justice with others of diverse experience, talents and background.

Chapter 5

Decision-making

'Make up your mind' is an injunction which can sometimes be ignored, sometimes postponed. It is inescapable for the magistrate. Courts must adjudicate. Adjournments for a social inquiry report or the deferment of sentence should never be a way of putting off the final decision.

While decision-making is the responsibility of the bench alone, it remains the hallmark of a competent chairman to know when he needs to seek the clerk's advice on matters of practice, procedure and law. On a proper understanding of this partnership between lay and legally qualified the calibre of the bench depends. We have therefore outlined principles and information basic to decision-making on bail, verdict, sentence and ancillary orders. This is readily available from the clerk, but nevertheless if the chairman has it at his finger-tips he will be more sure-footed in structuring discussion and more alert to the need for further advice from the clerk in a particular case.

Decision-making is no more the prerogative of the chairman than of each of his colleagues, however newly appointed, but inevitably he has a key role in the decision-making process. Few judicial decisions can be more important than sentences. They reflect a person's past conduct in a way which has a controlling influence on his future and in the aggregate have a decisive effect on the well-being and safety of the public. The responsibility of the bench when deciding, for instance, whether or not to deprive a defendant of his liberty can never be taken lightly, particularly when the offender is facing a first custodial sentence.

We examine judicial decision-making under eight headings: (1) Bail, (2) Verdict, (3) Sentence, (4) Sentencing options, (5) Deferment of sentence, (6) Preventive justice, (7) Ancillary orders, and (8) Consistency in sentencing.

(1) BAIL

Under the Bail Act 1976 all defendants are entitled to unconditional bail. This right can be removed on stated grounds for specific reasons. A record of both must be kept and a copy handed to the defendant on his request. The way in which bail decisions are approached' varies considerably from court to court. A strong case can be made out for the adoption of a standard procedure. An example of such a procedure is set out in appendix V.

Chairmen should be familiar with the list of exceptions in paragraph 2 of Part I of Schedule 1 to the Bail Act 1976, on which the presumption of the right to bail can be rebutted. In taking decisions under paragraph 2 the court should have regard to considerations such as the nature and seriousness of the offence, the defendant's criminal record, his failure to surrender to custody in the past and the absence of a fixed abode.[1] It should be remembered that these are not in themselves 'exceptions' but rather considerations to be taken into account.

At the Magistrates' Association's Summer Training Conference in 1985, the 'expert' benches on the platform fell into the trap of giving 'the serious nature of the offence', 'no fixed abode', and 'bad record' as exceptions for refusing bail. Each of these may provide the 'substantial grounds for believing that one of the exceptions applies' (for example, that if released on bail the accused will fail to surrender to custody, commit an offence, or interfere with witnesses or otherwise obstruct the course of justice), but they are not themselves exceptions. The bench may have other considerations which are relevant to the decision on bail. The chairman should state clearly both the exceptions and the considerations in the reasons given without prompting from the clerk. Hesitation can give the impression that the bench falters when making decisions.

Any decision should be made only after a thorough investigation of all relevant matters. Bail is no exception. If, for example, the police request time to complete enquiries which are not practicable unless the defendant is in custody, the chairman should ask why this is the case and how long they are likely to need. The remand can be timed accordingly.

Magistrates no longer have a duty to reconsider a previous refusal of bail.[2] Once withheld, the adjudication stands, unless there is a change of circumstances such as in the family situation, sureties

1 Particularly on serious charges the chairman should press the prosecution to give information on these matters if it is not volunteered.

2 *R v Nottingham Justices, ex p Davies* [1980] 2 All ER 775.

coming forward, an offer of accommodation or of employment. The claimed change of circumstances can be tested in the witness box. The prelude to the application is often, 'He has been a long time on remand in custody'. Prolongation of the same circumstances is hardly a change.

Particular difficulties attend the decision on whether or not to grant bail. It is not based on the certainties of past conduct but involves a prediction as to the probabilities for future behaviour. Will the accused, if granted bail, surrender to custody, commit further offences, interfere with the course of justice, be likely to be the victim of attack? Moreover, the rules of evidence do not apply to a bail application and much of what the bench relies on to support its decision, is hearsay or opinion.

The bench is assisted in making up its mind in two ways. First, the likely future conduct of the accused on a grant of bail will reflect his past behaviour. If the accused has flouted the court's authority in the past by breaching a previous grant of bail, a suspended sentence or a condition order, without good reason, the court may well conclude that he is unlikely to comply with the conditions of an order for bail. Second, the gravity of the alleged offence. A distinction should be drawn between a lad who goes out equipped for a fishing expedition and succumbs to the sight of a purse on a kitchen table, spotted through an open back door, and a professional burglar going equipped for crime. A most important factor in deciding a bail application is the need to protect the public. Violence, actual or threatened, in the course of the alleged crime is a strong contraindication to the grant of bail.

Upon refusal of bail, an unrepresented defendant must be told of his right to apply for bail to the High Court. In two other circumstances he must be told of his right to apply for bail to the Crown Court. These are if:

(i) the court is committing him for trial at the Crown Court, or
(ii) the court issues a certificate that it heard full argument on the bail application.

A court is under a duty to issue a certificate when it remands a person in custody on the adjournment of an enquiry (that is, committal proceedings) or of a trial or for a medical report, after hearing full argument; and either (a) it has not previously heard such argument, or (b) having heard full argument before, the court is satisfied that there has been a change in circumstances or that new considerations have been placed before the court. The court must state in the certificate what are the changes in circumstances or the new considerations.

If a defendant is putting forward that there has been a change in circumstances or there are new considerations, the matter should be taken step by step. First the court should consider whether there has been a change in circumstances or there are new considerations. If the court decides there are not, that is the end of the matter. If the court decides there are, it should then go on to hear the full argument.

The accused may be in the dock during a bail application, but he remains innocent in the eyes of the law as long as he is unconvicted. The refusal of bail is not a punishment. The bench should be aware of the seriousness of depriving an unconvicted man of his liberty. Conditional bail should be considered as an alternative. Can it properly protect the public and allow an accused to retain his liberty? If so, grant it. Each condition is the result of an independent decision. The conditions most commonly considered are:

(a) reporting at stated intervals and times at a specified police station. Here the location of the alleged offence is pertinent. If in the city centre, it may be inept to require an offender who lives in the suburbs to report near the scene of his crime, possibly feeling he would like to recoup his bus fares;
(b) a curfew. This confines the offender, usually during hours of darkness. It has the advantage of enabling him to continue in daytime employment. It may be a more productive alternative than daily reporting at an already over-crowded police station;
(c) a surety or sureties. If present in court, sureties should be examined on oath and warned of the hazards. The chairman should advise them to contact the police if the conduct of the accused on bail makes them uneasy about his ultimate surrender to custody. If sureties are not present, the court may fix the amount of the recognisance and leave it to the police to approve. If it is feared that the accused may abscond abroad, in addition to the temporary forfeiture of his passport and the acceptance of sureties, he may be required to deposit a sum of money as security with the court, or with his solicitor to the order of the clerk of the court.

A particular problem arises when a notice of appeal against a custodial sentence has been given and an application is made to the bench for bail. In these circumstances bail should rarely be granted. The bench which imposed the custodial sentence will have thought that no other course was appropriate.

It is implicit in all decision making that justices should not only decide, but should look ahead to the consequences of their decision. To grant bail pending appeal would encourage hopeless appeals and efforts to postpone custody. Moreover, as the Court of Appeal has pointed out,[2] it imposes a heavy burden on them. Once bail is granted pending an appeal, judges who later hear it are presented with an additional problem. Bail inevitably raises hopes, and to wreck them by ordering a return to custody is a painful duty.

(2) VERDICT

Every chairman, on his own and his colleagues' account, will have wrestled with the standard of proof, proof beyond reasonable doubt in criminal cases and proof on the balance of probabilities in civil cases.

The standard of proof

BEYOND REASONABLE DOUBT

Lord Denning's explanation[3] of the burden of proof beyond reasonable doubt is an illuminating starting point:

> It need not reach certainty, but it must carry a high degree of probability. Proof beyond a reasonable doubt does not mean proof beyond the shadow of a doubt. The law would fail to protect the community if it admitted fanciful possibilities to deflect the course of justice. If the evidence is so strong against a man as to leave only a remote possibility in his favour, which can be dismissed with the sentence 'of course it is possible but not in the least probable', the case is proved beyond reasonable doubt, but nothing short of that will suffice.

The Specimen Directions to Judges (in summing-up to juries) prepared by Master D R Thompson, CB, QC, and his staff, at the request of the Judicial Studies Board and approved by the Lord Chief Justice, deal with the matter in this way:

> Before you can convict you must be satisfied so that you feel sure – which is the same thing as being satisfied beyond reasonable doubt – of the defendant's guilt.

A note to the section reads;

> Beyond this, no explanation of the meaning of reasonable doubt should be attempted.

That convinces us that we should attempt no further explanation.

2 *R v Gruffydd* (1972) 56 Cr App Rep 585.
3 *Miller v Minister of Pensions* [1947] 2 All ER 372.

THE BALANCE OF PROBABILITIES

In magistrates' courts the standard of proof on the balance of probabilities applies in civil cases and in criminal cases when the burden of proof shifts to the accused. For example, when an accused is charged with having done something without a licence and the prosecution has proved that something was done that required a licence and that the accused failed to produce the licence, the onus shifts to the defendant to prove, on the balance of probabilities, that he had a licence at the relevant time.

The Specimen Directions to Judges explain this as follows:

> It must carry a reasonable degree of probability, but not so high as is required in a criminal case. If the evidence is such that the tribunal can say: 'we think it more probable than not' the burden is discharged, but if the probabilities are equal it is not.

The standard of proof is the yardstick by which the magistrates decide on the verdict. There are many points to be considered. Was the plea unequivocal? Did the witness lie or was he telling the truth? A miscarriage of justice can arise if a lying witness is believed and an honest one ignored. What must the prosecution prove to make out its case? Magistrates should know the elements of the offence they are trying. If in doubt on these, the chairman needs to consult the clerk.

Before a magistrate can reach a verdict, he has to assess the evidence. He must keep an open mind until all the evidence has been given. He should beware of reaching a decision at the close of the prosecution's case unless it be that the prosecution has failed to make out a case which has to be answered.

A court will never get as far as a verdict if it upholds a submission that there is no case to answer. This is a searching piece of decision making. The High Court in a *Practice Note* (1962) gave the following guidance:

> A submission that there is no case to answer may properly be made and upheld (a) when there has been no evidence to prove an essential element in the alleged offence; (b) when the evidence adduced by the prosecution has been so discredited as a result of cross-examination or is so manifestly unreliable that no reasonable tribunal could safely convict on it.[4]

The bench will sift the significant from the unimportant, decide on the weight to be given to each piece of evidence and ensure that the evidence deals with all the elements of the alleged offence. The

4 [1962] All ER 448.

circumstances surrounding the alleged commission of the offence can be important. For example, in a road traffic case, weather, visibility, the configuration of the road, the viewpoint of a witness and the length of his observation, may all be relevant features of the case.

The magistrate should always proceed with caution, taking nothing for granted. If, as a result of a search warrant, an offensive weapon is found in the house of the accused, that discovery is not proof that he put it there. Did the store detective see the goods actually placed in the defendant's basket? In many cases, the only evidence is circumstantial, but equally the weight given to circumstantial evidence is not necessarily any less than that given to direct evidence.

Reaching a verdict is the culmination of a continuous decision-making process which will be as individual as the magistrates who embark upon it. The chairman should respect individuality but must also co-ordinate the collective decision.

(3) SENTENCE

The sentence is, for the convicted at any rate, the focal point of the proceedings. Magistrates have to come to terms with the fact that they are in the business of punishment. By this we mean the deprivation for another of one or more of his basic human rights, such as autonomy over his person or property. Deprivation is only judicial punishment when it is deserved. Punishment acknowledges that, generally speaking, normal people are responsible for their actions. This aspect of human dignity can be greatly prized. A defendant sometimes rejects probation in favour of 'punishment'.

If everyone were wholly responsible for his actions, the protection of the public well might be the only consideration in sentencing. A rigid tariff system would then be appropriate and many complexities of decision-making would be taken out of sentencing. But responsibility may be diminished by mental disability, by psychological disturbance, by personal circumstances, and by family, neighbourhood, or peer group environment.

It is, however, too deterministic to say human beings are necessarily victims of circumstance. In comparable situations some behave badly while the majority behave well. We cannot overlook deliberate, calculated offending and must be ready to diagnose it in court. Equally, mitigation and the claims of the offender are matters to be taken into account when deciding on sentence. We often have to assess blameworthiness rather than guilt in deciding how far the offence was deliberate and the degree to which responsibility was diminished. Here the probation service, through a social inquiry report, can give invaluable assistance.

In deciding on sentence, magistrates have a twofold duty: to protect the public, and to reflect genuine mitigating factors. These duties are included in the classic principles of sentencing:[5] retribution, deterrence, prevention and rehabilitation.

Disillusionment with deterrence and reform can encourage a fresh look at retribution. Individualised sentences framed on the 'treatment model' then give way to sentences based on the 'justice model'. These centralise the offence rather than the offender and predicate the tariff system. Magistrates should appraise calmly any move towards retribution which may be engendered by public panic. Once again, there is Appeal Court guidance. Courts should take public opinion into account but not pander to it, because it may be wrong-headed or sentimental.[6]

The classic principles of sentencing (above) are being extended to include reparation both as a principle and in practice, particularly since compensation became a penalty in its own right.[7]

We shall examine certain general practical problems in sentencing and then individual sentences, with reference to guidance from the High Court and recognised good practice in magistrates' courts.

General problems

CO-DEFENDANTS

Co-defendants should be dealt with in an even-handed manner but there is no principle in law that co-defendants should receive the same sentence. The circumstances of each individual are to be considered separately. It is no mitigation to claim that others, whether charged or not, are equally to blame. The sentence of each defendant will be decided by having regard to culpability for the immediate offence, any previous convictions and the complex of mitigating and other circumstances. A sentence passed on one co-defendant does not fix a ceiling for others. When considering financial penalties, the court must take into consideration the means of the offender so far as they appear or are known to the court.[8]

5 *R v Sergeant* [1975] Crim LR 173.
6 *R v Sergeant* (1975) 60 Cr App Rep 74.
7 Criminal Justice Act 1982, s 67.
8 Magistrates' Courts Act 1980, s 35.

THE COMPOSITION OF THE BENCH

It is highly desirable that the bench which convicts should also sentence. An adjournment for the preparation of a social inquiry report may render this impracticable. This is particularly unsatisfactory when there was a not guilty plea. The sentencing bench is then not aware of all the nuances of the case revealed to the trial bench.

The situation is covered by statute. 'The court which sentences or deals with him (the offender) need not be composed of the same justices as that which convicted him.'[9] It goes on to require that if the court consists of or includes anyone who was not present at the original hearing the court shall, before sentencing him, make such inquiry into the facts and circumstances of the case as will enable the justices who were not sitting when the offender was convicted to be fully acquainted with those facts and circumstances.

THE APPROACH TO SENTENCING

In striving to strike a balance between the magistrates' public duty to protect the community and the proper claims of the offender, we have found it helpful to ask the following questions:

(i) What is the gravity and nature of the offence?
(ii) What are the interests of the public?
(iii) Are there any circumstances of the offence which aggravate or mitigate the crime?
(iv) Do the answers to (i) and (ii) above indicate so small a threat to public safety that the interests of the accused can be taken into account?

This sequence paves the way to an individualised sentence, particularly within the range of non-custodial and rehabilitative disposals. The fourth consideration frequently applies in magistrates' courts where the less serious offences are dealt with. Many cases heard by magistrates require finely balanced decisions between custody and a sentence served in the community.

The bench must first distinguish between those who need help and those who deserve punishment. Repeated leniency breeds contempt. This can sometimes be the legacy of a series of appearances in the juvenile court. Magistrates should not sentence on record. To do so would amount to double jeopardy. Previous convictions can negate mitigation, indicate the likely effectiveness of a future sentence, or suggest an alternative. Some factors

9 Magistrates' Courts Act 1980, s 121 (7).

paraded as mitigation, 'I was drunk at the time', are rarely to be regarded. A diminution of responsibility as a result of self-induced intoxication – a common excuse – is not a ground for mitigating punishment.

Genuinely mitigating factors include:

(i) the good character of the defendant,
(ii) his age. Is he, for instance, in his teens or approaching old age?
(iii) whether he was provoked,
(iv) personal difficulties of family, finance or employment,
(v) disability,
(vi) a plea of guilty.

The defendant should be given credit for a guilty plea, which saves court time, saves witnesses the stress of attending court and giving evidence, and saves public funds. A guilty plea may also indicate contrition, as would assisting the police to recover goods. While sentence should not be increased because of a not guilty plea, there can often and properly be a more lenient approach where there is a plea of guilty. There is a helpful note on the subject in *The Magistrate*.[10]

(4) SENTENCING OPTIONS

The art of sentencing is fitting the punishment to the crime and the criminal. The great divide in sentencing lies between the custodial and non-custodial disposal. Attention has been focused on overlong custodial sentences and overcrowding in prisons. Research has raised doubts about the effectiveness of custody as a means of reducing recidivism. There is convincing evidence that the shock of the 'clang of the prison gates' diminishes as the offender adapts to his circumstances. It follows that in many cases a short prison sentence is as effective as a long one.

If reform is hoped for, a custodial sentence may not be appropriate. Exchanging a name for a number is hardly conducive to reforming one's way of life and it is difficult to teach the proper use of freedom to those in custody. Learning how to use free time is important since crime is predominantly a leisure time activity of the young.

Immediate custodial sentences

An immediate custodial sentence should only be passed if no other disposal meets the seriousness of the offence and the circumstances

10 (1985) 41 The Magistrate at p 146.

of the offender. It should be as short as possible, consistent with the protection of the public and the need to deter the criminal.[11] It should never be used as a substitute for a fine for those of small means. It should not be lengthened because of remission. It is rarely suitable for trivial offences even if the defendant has a bad record.[12]

On occasions an exemplary sentence is appropriate. It overrides individual considerations, so there are ethical problems in punishing a person more severely than his crime would warrant as a warning to others. The exemplary sentence is at its most effective when a particular crime is holding a locality to ransom. This may occur, for example, when frequent offences of violence accompany football matches. An exemplary sentence will almost certainly be one of immediate custody or a heavy fine.

Where more than one offence has been committed by a single defendant, each meriting custody, magistrates must decide whether to make the sentences concurrent or consecutive. If the offences arise out of the same transaction, or there are a series of similar offences, then concurrent sentences are indicated. If, however, an accused has stolen tools in order to break and enter, those two offences are not to be regarded as part of the same transaction. Where offences are dissimilar, committed on different occasions or during the operational period of a suspended sentence or probation order, or while on licence or on bail, consecutive sentences should generally be imposed.

The suspended sentence

To suspend a custodial sentence may be appropriate where the gravity of the offence indicates custody but the circumstances of the offender suggest that he may respond to the threat of custody. If a suspended sentence is breached, then in normal circumstances the sentence should be activated. The sentencing court is not, however, a rubber stamp. It will review the circumstances before activating a suspended sentence, and may refrain from doing so if it would be unjust. It would be wrong to do so when the new offence is trivial or different in character. If the breach occurs towards the end of a period of suspension, the court may well activate the sentence, but for a reduced term. If custodial penalties for both the suspended sentence and the new offence would together be excessive, justices will use their discretion to adjust one or both. Chairmen should check with the clerk that the new offence is punishable with

11 *R v Bibi* [1980] 1 WLR 1193.
12 *R v Upton* (1980) 124 Sol Jo 359.

imprisonment, and to confirm that the court has power to activate the suspended sentence. If a conditional discharge or a probation order is made on the present offence, it is not a conviction, and the question of activating the suspended sentence will not arise.

It is possible to impose a fine with a suspended sentence of imprisonment. It is important that a fine should not appear as the punishment while a suspended sentence is regarded as a let-off. If a fine alone is the right sentence, pass it.

The partly suspended sentence

In view of the maximum length of custodial sentence available to magistrates, this is less useful to magistrates than to the higher courts. No sentence should be extended in length because it is partly suspended.

Lord Lane, as Lord Chief Justice, has given guidance[13] as to the use of a partly suspended sentence. He says that, before imposing a partly suspended sentence, the court should ask itself:

(i) Is it a case where a custodial sentence is really necessary?
(ii) If it is necessary, can a community service order be made as an equivalent to imprisonment, or can the court suspend the whole sentence?
(iii) If neither is appropriate, what is the shortest sentence the court can properly impose?

If imprisonment is necessary, and if a very short sentence is not enough, and if it is not appropriate to suspend the sentence altogether, then partial suspension should be considered.

Community service orders

Community service orders are only available for imprisonable offences. They highlight two very different approaches to sentencing. When considering making a community service order, some magistrates ask, 'Is custody appropriate in this case?' followed by, 'Are there nevertheless factors which enable us to consider community service as an alternative?' Others maintain that, having had the statutorily required report as to the defendant's suitability for a community service order and the availability of work, it can be used as an order in its own right. A request for a report as to the suitability of a defendant for community service inevitably raises his expectations. If it is requested by the court, its recommendations

13 *R v Clarke* [1982] 3 All ER 232.

should be followed[14] unless the chairman has stated that it, or any bench on the adjourned hearing, may decide on another disposal. The community service order, with its opportunity for reparation to the community, is a constructive and hopeful sentence. It is administered by the probation service, which matches the offender to his work and has overall responsibility for him.

Community service orders can be particularly appropriate for young offenders who may yet be deterred from a life of crime, or for recidivists whose offences are principally a nuisance to the community.

The potential advantage of a community service order cuts two ways: the offender may be in therapeutic contact with those responsible for the work project on which he is placed, such as the warden of an old people's home or the leader of a club for the disabled; thus members of the community may learn that the protection of the public from crime requires their participation. Moreover, the offender, especially in a project where he is helpful to individuals, may realise, perhaps for the first time in his life, that it matters to somebody else how he behaves. This is not a bad antidote to crime.

Monetary penalties

FINES

Fines in the magistrates' court rise to a maximum of £2,000 for level 5 offences. When exercising its wide discretion as to the amount of a fine, the court should have the following points in mind. It should be fixed in relation to the gravity of the offence and mitigated for offenders of limited means. It must be enforceable, and where it is being imposed for more than one offence it should take account of the total amount a defendant can pay. A fine should never become an alternative route to prison for those who cannot, with reasonable sacrifice, be expected to keep up their instalments. It should be high enough to deter and yet not be beyond the means of the defendant. Although superficially attractive, it is probably wrong to impose a fine which represents the average of the amounts proposed by the individual members of the bench. The amount of a fine is better fixed by thorough discussion until a decision emerges.

COMPENSATION

It is often said that courts do not pay sufficient regard to the interests of victims. It is also said that magistrates do not make full use of their power to award compensation.

14 *R v Gillam* [1981] Crim LR 55.

Chairmen should therefore be alert to the fact that a compensation order may be made on conviction whether or not an application is made on behalf of the victim. Two changes brought about by the Criminal Justice Act 1982 point to the weight placed by Parliament on the value of a compensation order in providing speedy redress for a victim who has suffered injury, damage or loss as a result of a crime. Firstly, since 31 January 1983 courts have been able to order the payment of compensation as the sole or main penalty for an offence. In 1985 about 3% of the total number of compensation orders made were of this kind. Secondly, where a court considers that both a fine and compensation are appropriate, but the defendant has insufficient means to pay both in full, the court must give preference to compensation.

The amount of compensation that may be ordered is up to £2,000 for each offence on which a conviction is recorded. So if there are four such offences the compensation may be up to £8,000. If offences are taken into consideration compensation may be awarded on them as long as the total sum, determined by the number of offences on which convictions are recorded, is not exceeded.

The assessment of the appropriate amount of compensation is usually relatively easy in cases of theft and criminal damage, but more difficult in cases of personal injury. Of assistance in this regard are the Magistrates' Association's guidelines *'Compensation for Personal Injury'*. The third edition of these was published at page 95 of the May 1984 issue of *'The Magistrate'*.

Magistrates' powers to order compensation are not as wide as would appear to be the case at first sight, in that the higher courts have laid down that compensation orders should only be made in clear, simple and uncomplicated cases, where there is convincing evidence of the fairness and accuracy of the claim. In other cases it should be left to the civil courts.

Sadly, in many cases the limited means of defendants do not permit the making of the kind of compensation order that the justice of the case merits. It is however important to make a realistic order rather than one that raises the hopes of a victim and then dashes them to the ground when it becomes obvious that the sum ordered is beyond the means of the defendant.

Orders on conviction

These include:

THE ABSOLUTE DISCHARGE

This amounts to an unconditional discharge. It is particularly appropriate where the offence is trivial, where either no culpability attaches to the offender, or he committed the offence unintentionally, and the court considers it inexpedient to inflict punishment. It should not usually follow deliberate offending.

THE CONDITIONAL DISCHARGE

This is applicable where it is inexpedient to punish and probation is not appropriate, but a condition of not re-offending is a necessary adjunct to the court's order. It is sometimes a good sentence for the first time offender who has committed a minor offence which is too serious to go totally unmarked by the court but who is unlikely to re-offend. If the offender breaches the order, the court may deal with him in any way it could have done for the original offence. This is a valuable and under-used order. Its effectiveness would be much enhanced if breaches were dealt with significantly.

THE PROBATION ORDER

Unadorned this is useful for the first time offenders whom the court feels require help in order not to re-offend. During the term of the probation order the needs of the offender, as they unfold, can be referred to an officer who in case or in group work is there to 'advise, assist and befriend' him.[15] For more serious offenders a more structured probation order is required. Conditions can be attached, for example that the offender should attend a day centre, or an alcohol unit or a group, on specified occasions. Specific conditions facilitate the identification of breach and the decision on the appropriate course to adopt if the matter is brought back to court. An offender should not usually be put on probation without the court first receiving a social inquiry report.

SOCIAL INQUIRY REPORT

A social inquiry report may be prepared to assist the magistrates in deciding on a wide range of sentences. Where it is discretionary the justices should always be able to justify the need for a report, in specific terms, before requiring one. Much information can be gained during the case from police antecedents and from the speech in mitigation. A report should never be requested merely because a bench cannot make up its mind and is casting its burden on another sentencing court.

When magistrates need more information before passing sentence, the report should reveal the offender to the court, address

15 Probation Rules 1984, SI 1984/647, r 33(a).

itself to specific problems such as alcoholism or drug addiction and be able to give some background of the offence and indicate the attitude of the offender to its commission. When ordering a report, the chairman should give guidance in court to the probation service as to any specific area of inquiry which will maximise its usefulness in deciding on the ultimate disposal. See p 16 for the value of 'stand-down' reports.

(5) DEFERMENT OF SENTENCE

Deferment of sentence (not 'passing a deferred sentence') is a power available to the courts since 1973.[16] It is limited to one period of deferment only, which must not exceed six months. The power is exercisable only with the consent of the offender and if it serves the interests of justice. It is intended to give an opportunity to take account of the conduct of the offender after some expected change in his circumstances, such as marriage, parenthood, employment, or a reduction in drug dependence. The court must be clear in its own mind why it is deferring sentence. The chairman must make its reasons known to the offender and tell him how it hopes to be made aware of the effect, if any, a change in his circumstances has had on his behaviour. Evidence of this may be by a probation report, wages slips, or reference from his employer.

No supervision attaches to a period of deferment. If immediate supervision were called for, a probation order would be more appropriate. When the defendant re-appears to be sentenced at the end of the period of deferment, he should be given full credit for any remedial steps which he has achieved. A custodial sentence is not appropriate if he has substantially complied with the court's expectations.[17]

(6) PREVENTIVE JUSTICE

A magistrate's power to bind over a person to keep the peace or be of good behaviour derives from common law, his Commission and statute law. It can name a person towards whom peaceable behaviour is specifically enjoined. Binding over is useful but should not be over-used. It can be valuable where there are sound judicial reasons for believing that the person's future conduct can be

16 Powers of Criminal Courts Act 1973, s(1).
17 *R v Smith* (1979) 1 Cr App Rep (S) 339.

restrained, and, if so restrained, that a breach of the peace is unlikely to recur. It will only be effective for those with powers of self-control. A kerb crawler might be deterred where an alcoholic might not. The court can, in its discretion, require a surety for the exacting task of ensuring good behaviour during the period of the bind-over.

(7) ANCILLARY ORDERS

In its anxiety to impose the right sentence, it is easy for a court to overlook the ancillary orders. This can lead to injustice. When, for instance, the court has announced financial penalties totalling £200 for a number of offences, and the prosecutor then successfully applies for £100 to cover a doctor's fee and plan and witness expenses in addition to his own costs, or an order of disqualification for driving is added as an afterthought, undue hardship may be caused to a defendant. A 'split' order should be avoided. In *R v Talgarth Justices, ex p Bithell*[18] magistrates were held to be wrong in imposing a fine on one day and a disqualification on a later date.

Costs

This has been a controversial subject. The time-honoured policy of the Magistrates' Association[19] has been to urge that the law should be amended to provide that all the costs of a criminal case should be met from government funds. But the introduction of the Crown Prosecution Service[20] has brought fundamental changes and there now seems no prospect of achieving the Association's aims. The new Service is publicly funded: a prosecutor appearing for the service will seek costs against a convicted defendant, not from public funds. Many defendants appearing before magistrates have very limited resources so a global approach to the allocation of these resources, between compensation, fine, and costs is a sensible one. Compensation now takes priority; a fine comes second; and very often it will be what is left over that goes to costs.

Costs should be kept in step with any fine imposed. It has also been held to be wrong in principle to order costs in such an amount that a defendant is unable to pay within a reasonable time of about twelve months.[1]

18 [1973] 2 All ER 717.
19 Annual Report 1974-5, appendix VI.
20 Prosecution of Offences Act 1985.
1 *R v Nottingham Justices, ex p Fohmann*, Queen's Bench Division, October 23, 1986.

Costs ordered by magistrates may be either *between parties* or from *central (that is, government) funds*. Several important changes in this regard have been effected by the Prosecution of Offences Act 1985. An award may still be made between parties but only against the defendant, on conviction. However, a successful defendant in a summary case, say, careless driving or speeding, may now be awarded costs from central funds. Formerly such an award could only be made in an indictable case. An award of costs out of central funds may not be made to the Crown Prosecution Service or a public authority. It will however still be possible to award costs out of central funds to a private prosecutor.

An award to a defendant of costs out of central funds is known as a 'defendant's costs order'. It will generally be appropriate to make an order for the full costs of the defendant when the case is dismissed or not proceeded with. The principles to be followed will be similar to those laid down in a practice note by the Lord Chief Justice in 1982.[2] The amount of any order will either be fixed at the time of the hearing if it can then be agreed, or be left to be assessed by the clerk later.

Restitution

Chairmen should not confuse restitution with compensation. The power of restitution is not much used in magistrates' courts. The law involved is complex. Furthermore, it is settled law that restitution orders should only be made in certain prescribed circumstances. Section 28 of the Theft Act 1968 gives the power to make an order for restitution when:

(1) Goods have been stolen or obtained by deception or blackmail.
(2) The offender is convicted of any offence with reference to the theft, whether or not stealing is the gist of the offence.
(3) The offender is convicted of any other offence but an offence under (2) is taken into consideration.
(4) In the court's opinion the relevant facts are sufficiently clear from evidence given at the trial or from the available documents (that is, admissible written statements or admissions).

The court may make several kinds of order in seeking to redress the wrong done to losers. The court may order anyone having possession or control of stolen goods to restore them to any person entitled to them. If the goods have been disposed of the court may, on the application of a person entitled to the goods, order the

2 *Practice Note* [1982] 3 All ER 1152 (see Appendix VI).

delivery or transfer of goods representing the proceeds of the disposal. If money was taken from the offender on his apprehension, the court may order a sum, not exceeding the value of the stolen goods, to be paid to the loser.

If someone has purchased stolen goods in good faith, the court may order that he be paid an amount up to the purchase price out of any money taken from the offender on his apprehension. A simple example would be where A steals B's car and sells it to an innocent purchaser C for £500, which is found on A when he is apprehended. Having convicted A of theft, the court may order C to restore the car to B, and may order A to pay £500 to C.

Where there is a dispute as to ownership, the matter should be left for the civil courts or the police using the procedures under the Police (Property) Act 1897.

Forfeiture

Powers of forfeiture are contained in numerous statutes. The most common concern dangerous drugs, firearms and offensive weapons, but there are also powers in respect of many other articles. It is necessary to consult the clerk as to the specific provision in each case, as the circumstances in which an order can be made vary considerably.

Deprivation

When an offender has used any property for the purpose of committing or facilitating the commission of an offence, the Powers of Criminal Courts Act 1973, section 43 provides a power for a court to deprive him of his rights in the property: but it is limited. The offence of which he is convicted must be one carrying two years or more imprisonment on indictment, such as theft or burglary. More importantly, it will only be appropriate for magistrates to use the power in simple cases where there is clear evidence to justify an order. It may be appropriate to deprive the offender of, for example, a motor car used in burglary. The effect of the order will be to place the property in police hands and they may thereafter take appropriate action under the Police (Property) Act 1897.

Disqualification and endorsement of driving licence

The main offences in respect of which a court must disqualify (in the absence of special reasons), or may disqualify and must endorse (in the absence of special reasons), are set out in The Magistrates'

Association's *Suggestions for Traffic Offence Penalties*.[3] All disqualifications will run from the time they are announced. It is no longer possible to make one disqualification run consecutive to another; nor may a disqualification be restricted to classes or types of vehicles.

THE PENALTY POINTS SYSTEM

If on conviction a defendant has twelve or more penalty points to be taken into account, the court is required to disqualify him for six months, unless there are grounds for mitigating the consequences.

There are four offences only which incur a variable number of points, namely, failing to stop after an accident, failing to report an accident, careless driving, and using a vehicle without third party insurance. When there are several offences, the correct number of points to be imposed is that for the offence which has the highest number of points. If one of the offences carries variable points, the court should first fix the number of points for this offence. There has been some difference of view as to whether it is right for the bench to look at the driving licence before deciding the number of points in such a case.

In the Magistrates' Association paper *The Penalty Points System* (Appendix VI, Annual Report 1982-3) the matter is set out as follows:

> *Offences carrying a variable number of points*
> It is the practice of some courts, when deciding the number of points to impose in respect of an offence carrying a variable number of points, not to look at the driving licence. This practice has its basis in the perfectly correct view that the primary consideration in deciding the number of points is the gravity of the offence. The chairman will ensure that his colleagues are aware that it is wrong for the court to increase the number of points it had in mind so as to render the defendant liable to penalty points disqualification, and equally wrong to reduce the number of penalty points in order to avoid having to impose a penalty points disqualification. The court is nevertheless under a legal obligation to see the licence before sentence, and should never increase or decrease points solely to disqualify or avoid disqualification. Previous endorsements are relevant where the offender has endorsements for similar offences to the present offence. In deciding how careless a defendant was, it may well be relevant to hear if he has previously been convicted of careless driving; in deciding the appropriate number of points for uninsured use, it may well be relevant to know whether he has previously been convicted for driving uninsured. It is therefore

3 Ninth edn, May 1985.

considered that a court should always look at the licence before finally deciding on the number of penalty points.

Any order of disqualification wipes the slate clean. This is a sensible and just provision in relation to a totting-up disqualification. It can, however, produce some curious results if a court wishes to impose a short period of disqualification but knows that in so doing all the points then on the licence will be wiped out. Another unfortunate consequence is that the DVLC computer at Swansea is literally wiped clean of the previous record. As most police forces no longer keep records of road traffic convictions, courts may be denied access to highly relevant information about previous convictions. The Annual General Meeting of the Magistrates' Association in October 1986 passed a resolution deploring this fact.[4]

SPECIAL REASONS AND MITIGATING CIRCUMSTANCES

It is important to understand the distinction between special reasons for not disqualifying and endorsing, and mitigating circumstances, in totting-up. Special reasons must relate to the circumstances of the offence and not the offender. In 1958 the following test as to what is a special reason was laid down in *R v Wickins*[5].

A special reason must:

(1) be a mitigating or extenuating circumstance;
(2) not amount in law to a defence;
(3) be directly connected with the commission of the offence;
(4) be a matter which the court ought properly to take into consideration when imposing sentence.

Examples of circumstances that have been found to be special reasons are that the defendant drove only a short distance, or that he was coping with an emergency. Personal circumstances of the defendant, such as his good driving record or the hardship he or his family would suffer if he were disqualified, cannot amount to special reasons. There is little room for finding special reasons in a drink/driving case. It is of course not a special reason that the defendant is only a small amount over the limit.

Magistrates have a wider discretion in assessing mitigating circumstances for not disqualifying a defendant under the totting-

4 (1987) 43 The Magistrate at p 7.
5 (1958) 42 Cr App Rep 236.

up provisions, or for disqualifying him for a shorter period than would normally be the case. The law under the Transport Act 1981, section 19(2) restricts the court's discretion more than was previously the case. Under the 1981 Act, if hardship is relied upon as part of mitigation, it must be shown to be exceptional, and magistrates may not take into consideration any circumstances which a defendant has successfully used within the previous three years to mitigate a totting-up disqualification. The relative triviality of the offence is not a mitigating circumstance.[6]

The onus is on the defendant to establish special reasons or mitigating circumstances on the balance of probabilities. The law requires the defendant to give or call evidence. Mere statements by his advocate, or by him not on oath, will not suffice.

If a court finds either special reasons or mitigating circumstances, the chairman must state the grounds for its order in open court and they are then recorded in the court register.

DISQUALIFICATION UNTIL TEST PASSED

The power should not be used as a punishment. Disqualification pending a test is appropriate if the court considers that because of age, infirmity or the circumstances of the offence, the defendant may not be a competent driver.[7]

(8) CONSISTENCY IN SENTENCING

Lord Lane has stated 'We are aiming at uniformity of approach to sentencing.'[8] The words, 'of approach to' are vital. We aim at consensus on principles of sentencing, but uniformity of sentencing would amount to injustice, unless of course we adopted the justice model and applied a tariff to each offence. Individualised sentencing is a fertile source of disparities which nevertheless can be consistent with justice. Potential injustice from inconsistency arises, for example, when there is a wide range of sentences for similar offences, such as road traffic offences. Chairmen can play a key role in aiming for consistency. They know the level of sentencing for particular offences in their locality and farther afield. The Magistrates' Association has outlined twenty-one ways of tackling the problem.[9] The Association also publishes its

6 The new 'totting' disqualification, (1984) 40 The Magistrate, at p 123.
7 Pending passing a further driving test: (1985) 41 The Magistrate, at p 162.
8 *R v Bibi* [1980] 1 WLR 1193.
9 Annual Report 1978-9, paper on Consistency in Sentencing.

Suggestions for Road Traffic Penalties as a starting point for deciding penalties for first offenders in average cases.

There are many important ingredients in decision-making in court. The chairman should be aware of these. The limits of the court's powers are set by statute. Within them the High Court gives unifying guidance which is binding on magistrates.

The discretion open to magistrates increases as sentencing options proliferate. However circumscribed the final decision of the court, decision-making remains the personal responsibility of the chairman and his colleagues. It will reflect their apprehension of the unique circumstances of the offender and the offence.

Chapter 6

Pronouncements in court

Announcing the decisions of the court is the exclusive and inescapable task of the chairman. How he does this should reflect their import in law as well as their significance for the individuals to whom they are directed and for the community whose protection is at stake.

PREPARATION

It is of the nature of our criminal justice system that it puts into the hands of magistrates a compass rather than a map of the path they should tread. It is understandable that chairmen reach for the map in the form of a rubric, for the pronouncement of sentence. This will ensure minimum standards. A chairman, however, should only resort to the recitation, or worse the reading aloud, of the prescribed rubric if all else has failed.

Pronouncement requires particular skills which have to be mastered. Training in chairmanship highlights the importance of the pronouncement in court. An experienced chairman should be sensitive to the natural apprehensiveness of a newcomer to the chair and be ready to advise. Practical assistance can result from the study of a form of words appropriate to each pronouncement and from an analysis of its essential ingredients (appendix VII). Proceedings can be invalidated if any one of them is omitted. A good insurance against this lies in a mental checklist.

Reading aloud the precise words of prescribed pronouncements is to be discouraged. The formal phraseology of the words may put their meaning beyond the reach of the defendant, to whom the verdict and the sentence are the most important points of the hearing. Each pronouncement needs to be adjusted to the comprehension of the defendant. If the chairman is studying the crib when making the pronouncements, he and his colleagues may appear to the defendant to lack faith in their conclusions.

The bench should have, and should be seen to have, confidence in their decisions. The best way to achieve this impression is for the chairman and his colleagues to face the defendant and give him the opportunity to return the courtesy. A view mainly of greying hair and receding hairline may do little to impress him when he has met the weight of the criminal justice system in action.

PRONOUNCEMENTS PRELIMINARY TO TRIAL

A number of pronouncements precede trial. On adjournment or remand, the fewer the words the better, provided all the statutory requirements are met. Prominence should be given to the statement of the time and place of the resumed hearing. If the adjournment is sine die, it may be necessary to explain that this means 'without a date having been fixed'.

Conditions of bail must be unambiguous. Understanding is necessary for compliance. When granting bail, a clear warning of the financial and custodial penalties for a breach of the conditions, or failure to surrender to bail at the stated time, should be given. A surety should be warned as to his responsibilities for the appearance of the accused on the appointed date (appendix VII). When the remand is in custody, the relevant statutory exceptions to a remand on bail must be unequivocally stated and the reasons for applying them clearly given and recorded.

The old style committal proceedings[1] require chairman and clerk to dovetail their functions in making pronouncements. We suggest the following:

(1) If the answer to the clerk's question as to whether reporting restrictions should be lifted is in the affirmative, the examining justice will announce his order that reporting restrictions are removed.
(2) After defence submissions, the magistrate rules either that there is no case to answer and instructs the accused that he is discharged, or that a prima facie case has been made out, when
(3) he will commit the defendant to stand his trial at the Crown Court, specifying whether on bail or in custody.
(4) Finally, he will respond to applications for witness orders, costs and legal aid.

1 Magistrates' Courts Act 1980, s 6(1).

Agreement between the chairman and the clerk as to how their interwoven functions are to be performed can minimise confusion and the need for the clerk to prompt the chairman. Under the shortened form of committal proceedings provided by the Magistrates' Courts Act 1980, section 6(2), the examining justice's part can be confined to the pronouncement of committal to the Crown Court and the decision on bail, witness orders, costs and legal aid. The examining justice should be prepared to explain terms to the accused. 'Alibi', for instance, is an unfamiliar word to some defendants. If the alibi warning is not understood and an explanation is not forthcoming from the clerk, the presiding magistrate should intervene with a clear definition.

VERDICT AND SENTENCE

For the bench, the climax of their endeavours is the decision on verdict and the consequent sentence. For those to whom these have not yet been announced, the critical focal point is to come. The chairman is the link between the two. If the bench has retired, on return to court the chairman will see his colleagues have settled and he has the full attention of the court before pronouncing verdict or sentence. He should be audible to everyone in the courtroom. He would do well to observe three golden rules – be clear, be concise, be correct. The chairman should make sure that his pronouncement has been fully understood by the defendant. Homilies are rarely assimilated. Nevertheless, it is sometimes appropriate for the bench to express the public's concern or displeasure.

In pronouncing verdict or sentence, the chairman is exercising a collective role. 'We' is appropriate because the whole bench or a majority of them should have formulated the utterance of one mouth. In a complicated case, the chairman should suggest the content and phraseology of anything he proposes to say, in explanation of verdict or sentence, in the retiring room. There the form in which it is to be delivered can be agreed with his colleagues. Care must be taken in phrasing a statement. Wrongly worded pronouncements may give rise to criticism or appeal. Therefore it is sound practice to tell the clerk what it is proposed shall be said and invite him to comment.

It is, of course, safe and easy for the chairman to say nothing beyond the bare facts. Hazards attend explanation. Equally, the law should be comprehensible to those required to live under it, and there are cases where some explanation is called for. Thus, unenlightened criticism can be replaced by public confidence in the administration of justice.

Different considerations often apply to the pronouncements of verdict and sentence, particularly when deciding whether or not to give reasons. When a defendant has advanced a spirited defence, it is usually appropriate for the bench to announce why it has found against him. Solicitors have been known to adjudge failure to do so as either discourteous or an adverse reflection on their own competence.

Verdict: reasons

Generally speaking, reasons should only be given for the verdict when exceptional circumstances require them. Brevity in pronouncing it is a good basic guide. 'We find you guilty' or 'not guilty' is more direct and comprehensible than 'We find the case proved' or 'We find that the case against you has not been proved'. The verdict should never be expanded by apology as in 'We reluctantly find the case against you has been proved'.

In spite of what has been said above, the Magistrates' Association has been opposed to stating reasons for conviction, being loath to risk giving grounds for appeal against a sound verdict.

An intense discussion followed the publication of a memorandum entitled *The Law and Practice on Appeals from the Criminal Jurisdiction of Magistrates' Courts* by the Law Society's Standing Committee on Criminal Law in 1971. It urged magistrates to give reasons on conviction as well as sentence, arguing that 'it is self evident that a defendant who has been convicted and is minded to appeal is entitled to know the reasons for the finding of guilt against him.' In addition, the absence of reasons makes it difficult to know whether the case was decided on fact, in which case an appeal should be to the Crown Court for re-hearing, or on law, in which case it should be directed to the Divisional Court on a case stated. These arguments have force. However, if a conviction is not appealable on the facts, magistrates may question the wisdom of creating the opportunity for a defendant to appeal on the reasons.

The main question for the chairman and his colleagues when deciding whether to give reasons or not will be whether the cause of justice would be furthered by an explanation, and whether reasons are necessary to meet the defendant's right to understand the law under which he is convicted. An explanation can make all the difference between acceptance of a verdict and grievance because of it. A defendant who has not grasped that there is a right of way over his land because he relied on a sketch plan presented at the time of purchase and has not realised that the OS map is the definitive authority, might, after explanation, realise that he had been justly treated. Similarly, an indication that contributory negligence is not relevant to an allegation of careless driving might remove some of the sting.

Having decided what reasons are to be given, if any, the wording should be scrutinised and extraneous or misleading material removed. Here the clerk's advice can be indispensable.

'We have considered your case most carefully' should go without saying. Chairmen need to make clear, brief statements with confidence and finality.

Sentence: reasons

In dealing with all but minor cases, there is a growing feeling that the bench should usually include reasons. Deciding what they should be concentrates the mind on the appropriateness of the sentence.

The Magistrates' Association cautiously opened the door to the giving of reasons for sentence in 1968. Then its Council resolved that whether or not it was desirable to give reasons in a particular case was at the discretion of the bench, which might see fit to explain an exceptionally light or heavy sentence. A defendant and the public are entitled to know when, for instance, apparent leniency reflects material in a social inquiry report which is not disclosed in open court, or when apparent severity is accounted for by an exemplary or deterrent sentence. Similarly, severity of sentence may result from the persistent disregard of repeated warnings. A rash of newspaper boys, undeterred by police warnings, riding on pavements to the danger of the blind, the handicapped, the old and the young, might incur a heavier penalty than the mere statement of the offence appeared to warrant. The sentence would exemplify the controlling influence a court can exercise on aspects of well-being in a neighbourhood.

A court is required to give reasons when sentencing a person under 21 to custody,[2] or anyone over that age to imprisonment for the first time.[3] The increase in sentencing options requires greater precision in sentencing and a need for clarity of reasoning which, when appropriate, can be disclosed in open court. Disclosure of reasons can reveal the purpose of a sentence and may encourage co-operation from the defendant in making it effective.

2 Criminal Justice Act 1982, s 2.
3 Powers of Criminal Courts Act 1983, s 20.

Justices should not feel constrained to give reasons every time they pass sentence. They can well omit them when they are implicit, as in disposals which require the defendant's assent, such as probation. In these disposals, reasons will emerge as the chairman outlines the statutory conditions and imposes discretionary conditions. Justices should give reasons for committing an offender to be sentenced by the Crown Court.

Reasons for sentence can often be quickly agreed by the bench. At other times, the chairman may have to reconcile two or three conflicting views. In the former case, the reasons are likely to be self evident, in the latter they will be the product of close argument. A decision has then to be made as to which, if any, of the reasons discussed are to be announced in court. Apart from mandatory requirements, reasons usually disclosed are likely to be those set out in the guidelines laid down by the Magistrates' Association in 1968 (p 62).

Sentence: pronouncement

The pronouncement of the sentence should be straightforward. In pronouncing a suspended or partially suspended custodial sentence, the temptation to postpone any mention of the suspended element to the end should be resisted. The punishment is not to be increased by creating unnecessary suspense in the imposition of a sentence. Reference may well be made to the offence, the record, and the reasons for considering immediate custody, followed straight away by the decision to suspend its operation.

If the defendant has cause to expect an immediate custodial sentence, reasons for its suspension should be given. The pronouncement could run as follows: 'Mr Smith, you have committed a serious offence and you have a bad record. We have considered immediate custody. However, we feel able to suspend the sentence in your case. In reaching this decision, we have given credit for your plea of guilty. We note that you have kept out of trouble for the last three years, and that you committed this offence while under considerable emotional stress. You are in work, and though that in itself is not a reason for our decision, it should persuade you not to re-offend. We are therefore imposing a sentence of 24 weeks imprisonment which will be suspended for two years.' The chairman then goes on to explain the implications of the sentence.

It is fairer to pronounce the term of a custodial sentence in days or weeks rather than in months, since this negates the effect of the different number of days in different calendar months. It also encourages fine tuning in the length of the sentence.

Every sentence should have been decided upon for cogent reasons. They are different in each case and these differences should be clearly reflected in the pronouncement. A few examples may illustrate this point.

Probation is an order which puts its recipient to the test over a set period of time. For up to three years a person can suffer considerable intervention in his personal autonomy while he has a penalty hanging over him for any infringement. The onerous nature of any fully implemented probation order can be increased by special conditions. These should be clearly defined and susceptible of supervision. If in doubt, the chairman can consult in open court with the duty probation officer before stating the conditions. It is the chairman's responsibility to see that all the implications of a probation order are clearly understood if the defendant's consent is to be valid.

Fine enforcement begins with the effectiveness with which the fine is assessed and announced. Before deciding to fine, the court is required to have regard to the defendant's means so far as they appear or are known to the court.[4] The bench having agreed the appropriate fine, the chairman should assume that it will be paid at once. When immediate payment is not offered, he should inquire whether the offender has any money at court and or whether he has any savings. If necessary, the chairman may order that the defendant be searched to ascertain whether he has any money with him. As a last resort, the bench should order payment over a period normally not exceeding twelve months, or by regular instalments during that time. The bench should never surrender the initiative but may permit the defendant to make an offer as to the period or instalments. The chairman should warn the defendant that custody can follow non-payment without due cause. Where fines are imposed for a series of offences, as in motoring cases, the chairman, having passed sentence on each offence separately, should state the total amount to be paid. This is particularly important if the fines are to be paid by instalments.

A fines enforcement court, conducted by a chairman who makes it clear that imprisonment follows failure to comply with the court's order, can act as a spur to the payment of fines.

There are pitfalls for the unwary in pronouncing sentence.

When other offences have been taken into consideration at the

4 Magistrates' Courts Act 1980, s 35.

defendant's request in deciding sentence, that fact should be announced as part of the court's adjudication.

Common omissions in the pronouncement of sentence include the failure of a chairman to explain different penalties passed on co-defendants. The difference will probably reflect differing degrees of culpability, or record, or differing claims in mitigation. Each co-defendant should at least understand the thinking behind disparate sentences, so that he may leave the court aware that he has had fair treatment.

Some chairmen have, when ordering a conditional discharge, been heard to say 'If you commit no other offence during the next twelve months, you will hear nothing further of this.' This comment is understandably tempting but is misleading because the order will be listed in any further disclosure of the defendant's antecedents, even though it was successfully concluded.

It is not safe for a chairman to tell a defendant that, in view of his record, he will never have another chance of avoiding a custodial sentence. He may have heard this on one or more previous appearances. The chairman can, however, couch his warning in such terms as: 'It is difficult to see how, if you commit any further offence, any bench could avoid imposing an immediate custodial sentence upon you.'

It is ill-advised to say, we only want to help you. This is a denial of the balance of criminal justice which must be maintained between the offender and those whom he has wronged.

It is unacceptable to make any comment which might appear to implicate the victim in the crime, such as deprecating the unlocked door, the transistor or the binoculars left unattended in full view on the car seat, or the goods on tempting open display in the shop. Such comment transfers blameworthiness from the offender to his victim, who may have been incautious but is innocent of the offence.

We no longer thunder homilies from the bench about past conduct. It is an exploitation of the chairman's position for him to go beyond the offences with which he is dealing, into general moral judgments. This does not mean that the chairman should never bring home the seriousness of dishonesty to a defendant whose record and reports show that he is one of those who regard theft as a justifiable redistribution of wealth. Indignation is inconsistent with the impartiality of justice and it is undesirable to widen the chasm between bench and dock by censoriousness.

The chairman, in agreement with his colleagues, can, when pronouncing sentence, express the hope that the defendant will see the sentence as a route to non-criminal conduct. This positive approach may help to prevent the waste of the defendant's time and the community's resources caused if he re-offends.

Chairmen should develop their individual style. Essential prerequisites are the prior study of a rubric, consultation with colleagues, and the advice of the clerk as to the availability, meaning and intention of a sentence. A chairman may have pronounced the same sentence scores of times before. He should remember that he is dealing with a defendant for whom this is 'his case'.

We are convinced that all chairmen in every one of our courts, held in about six hundred petty sessional divisions, could collectively enhance respect for law and order by the dignity, confidence, clarity and humanity with which they pronounce sentence. The effectiveness of any sentence, vital for the protection of the community and the future containment or well-being of the defendant, begins when the chairman pronounces it. The implications may be daunting. They should never be dodged. There is no substitute for experience, but reading, training and practice are some of the ways in which the chairman may master the art of the perfect pronouncement.

Chapter 7

The chairman's role in training

The quality of justice administered in the magistrates' courts depends on the calibre of each individual justice. Excellence derives from aptitude developed and directed by training. Justices are both born and made. They are culled from among their peers for a function the discharge of which can be decisive in the lives of many people. For their task they need all their innate ability buttressed by training and experience. Realising this, and busy as they are, magistrates are prepared to give their time to training.

INTRODUCTION TO TRAINING

A chairman's influence on colleagues less experienced than himself reflects his concept of his judicial role and his expertise in fulfilling it. A useful approach to his training task will include:

Recognition: that his colleagues are people of distinction and ability who, in many cases, hold prominent positions in which they render other service to the community. Each of these colleagues accepted office knowing that he would have to undertake a minimum of training. This initial training is often an eye-opener which, along with the responsibilities of office, underlines its relevance. Some whose appointment to the bench preceded the statutory requirement to train, are less ready to learn. They may believe that native wit and their own self-estimated common sense are adequate qualifications for the bench. While they conscientiously do their unaided best, the potential of training passes them by.

Preparation: By the time chairmen are contributing to the training of others, much of their own preparation for chairmanship will have been accomplished. Preparation includes practical experience, attending courses, and reading. Chairmen can draw on their own experience on the bench; their knowledge of the law; and their understanding of sentencing policy. The distillation of this experience and information can provide invaluable guidance to colleagues.

THE TRAINING TASK

Informal training

Much valuable training is gained sitting in court. The White Paper on 'The Training of Justices of the Peace in England and Wales' (Cmnd 2856) records that the overwhelming weight of opinion from experienced magistrates and their clerks was that experience on the bench was itself the finest form of training, and that theoretical training should be based on the foundation of practical experience.[1]

There is much to be said for practical experience as training, particularly in the early stages. No one should be better equipped than a chairman to contribute to this training with the problems and difficulties which arise during actual court experience well in mind. As in the professions, where experienced doctors, lawyers and teachers have an essential part in instruction, there is a strong case for chairmen to fulfil their role in practical as well as theoretical training. Informal training includes incidental assistance, observation in court, and attendance at meetings.

INCIDENTAL ASSISTANCE

Recently appointed justices have to get their eye in on a task which is probably unlike anything in their previous experience. They feel there is much to learn and all at once. The chairman may have to help a colleague through a crisis of confidence. Justified encouragement at the right moment can often overcome this. Over-confidence may be misguided or even border on arrogance which inhibits improvement.

Chairmen are more likely to need to act as a spur than a brake. They can encourage helpful, and discourage inappropriate, attitudes. It may be necessary to tell some colleagues that they cannot modify or apply the law as they would prefer it to be. In others, prejudice can override judgment. It can be consoling to find that we all have some bias arising out of our experience and beliefs,

1 (1982) 38 The Magistrate at p 3.

which has to be recognised and put to one side when making judicial decisions. In others, intuition can be a short cut to the wrong conclusion. It should always be checked by a steady and reasoned weighing of evidence. Many find it difficult to accept that the demands of justice are stern and rigorous. They can be mitigated by some qualities. Compassion has a place, but sentimentality none. A bench of magistrates is not a welfare committee though many decisions are made in which the welfare of the defendant has a part.

OBSERVATION IN COURT

Chairmen have a particular responsibility to new magistrates observing in court. This is part of the latters' statutory training, but formal preparation is difficult because it depends on the cases being heard on the day. It must be clear to everyone in court that observers are taking no part in the proceedings or deliberations. The following arrangements are appropriate when a newly appointed magistrate attends court as an observer:

(i) He should sit in the body of the courtroom so that he can observe the bench and the clerk, and if possible be accompanied by a senior magistrate or a member of the clerk's staff who will use the opportunity for commenting upon the proceedings and indicating matters of importance and interest at an appropriate time.
(ii) The magistrate must not take any part in the proceedings of the court.
(iii) He must not accompany the adjudicating magistrates if and when they retire to confer.
(iv) At the conclusion of each observation session, the magistrate should spend a period with the chairman and one or more of the adjudicating magistrates and the court clerk to give them an opportunity of explaining the proceedings of the court and answering questions.[2]

The value of observation can be greatly enhanced by apt direction from the chairman. Magistrates may never, subsequent to initial training, see their court from a public point of view. It is helpful to direct their attention to the potential insights from such observation. They could be asked to consider how, as magistrates in it, they could ensure that all those in court see that justice has been done.

If the visit to the court is the justice's first, it is helpful if the chairman ensures that he has sufficient introduction to the

2 *The Training of Magistrates* (Blue Book), Lord Chancellor's Dept, 1978.

proceedings to perceive what is happening, and to interpret it. The guidance given in the Blue Book[3] is helpful on this aspect of training.

Following observation, newly appointed magistrates appreciate an immediate post-court discussion with the chairman, his colleague justices and the clerk. This provides an opportunity for queries to be answered and for residual points to be raised by the bench and the clerk. The relevance of theoretical training is greatly enhanced when it follows hard on the heels of practical experience. The attention of the new magistrates may be drawn to the salient features of the court they have just observed.

The opportunity for new justices to test their opinions in discussion with those of longer experience is important. Temporary access to the documents in the cases, such as DVLC printouts and social inquiry reports, is permissible and can be illuminating.

MEETINGS

Bench meetings can be invaluable in training. Chairmen can involve willing newer members of the bench in deliberations. Participation may bring enlightenment. Taking a decision, for instance, on whether to adopt the Magistrates' Association's *Suggestions for Traffic Offence Penalties* or to apply other bench norms, can promote discussions on the level of sentencing for road traffic infringements compared with other offences, or the need to establish a reasonable level of consistency in sentencing throughout the country. These discussions, in the context of a bench meeting, highlight the relevance of such decisions on the bench for new magistrates.

Formal training

STATUTORY TRAINING

Magistrates' Courts Committees were first required to provide statutory training in 1949,[4] though their training programmes have extended beyond their statutory duty. Since 1 January 1966 justices have had to undergo Stage I and Stage II training. It has proved its worth in the growing confidence, accuracy, and stature of the magistracy. The 'Blue Book' states that in Stage I instruction will be provided by the clerk to the justices and/or the chairman of the

3 *The Training of Magistrates* (Blue Book), Lord Chancellor's Dept, 1978.
4 Justices of the Peace Act 1949.

bench or one of his experienced colleagues.[5] Many justices in training will agree that they fare best when the first 'or' is deleted.

Learning from experience never stops. There is need, however, to sustain the early enthusiasm for training. The 'Grey Book'[6] lays down guidelines for the Magistrates' Courts Committees concerning the in-service training which is required for those who have come to the bench since 1980. There is a choice of subjects in in-service training but training for chairmanship is one of the two which are obligatory. This underlines the importance of the role of the chairman.

NON-STATUTORY TRAINING

The independence of the judiciary is a vital element of the British constitution. It is maintained to no small degree by the non-statutory training which is provided under the auspices of the Magistrates' Association, founded in Guildhall, London, in 1920, for this purpose. Training occurs in its 59 Branches as well as nationally. This function is centralised in its charter and maintained with vigour. The training provided by the Association expounds what justices need to know and responds to what they want to know as a result of the problems which arise in the course of their jurisdiction. The Association is indebted to many supporters in lectures, courses, seminars and sentencing exercises. These programmes, however, would be incomplete without the involvement of experienced justices, usually chairmen, participating in discussion, chairing sentencing exercises, or speaking.

Following the report to the Lord Chancellor's Advisory Committee on the Training of Magistrates[7] by Sir Thomas Skyrme, a former Chairman of the Association's Council, the Lord Chancellor's Department finances the national training conferences of the Magistrates' Association. The subject matter, venue and date of these are announced in *The Magistrate*. They include much of value to potential and established chairmen. They are innovative both as to content and manner of presentation.

The involvement of chairmen in training complements the invaluable contributions of others, many of whom are lawyers. Clerks, in addition to their own expertise, have a particular insight into the magistrate's task. Members of the legal profession,

5 *The Training of Magistrates,* Lord Chancellor's Dept, 1978.
6 *Further Training for Magistrates* (Lord Chancellor's Dept).
7 Known as the Boreham Committee and recently replaced by The Judicial Studies Board.

academic lawyers, stipendiary magistrates, judges and ministers of state, also make a vital contribution to training. The opportunity to listen to those who work in other sectors of the penal system, specifically provided for in Part II of the basic training programme, is invaluable.

Training for chairmanship

The contribution of others is recognised by the Magistrates' Association, which nonetheless feels that the now obligatory training of chairmen cannot be properly achieved without the full participation of practising chairmen, with their day-to-day experience of what chairmanship involves. Training in chairmanship, organised by the Association, and involving established chairmen, has met with a good response from able magistrates and should be fostered.

COURSES IN TRAINING FOR CHAIRMANSHIP

The Magistrates' Association in 1984 set up the first of its courses to train established chairmen to participate in the training of prospective chairmen. Not every established chairman is expected to take part: it is well understood that not all feel they can contribute to this formal training. However, those who have communication skills are encouraged to assist in courses designed to be repeated in the Branches. These training courses employ methods and resources used in the teaching of adults in other fields and emphasise the development of communication techniques.

Training methods

The lecture, summarised in a written résumé and tested by question and discussion, is often accepted as the only approach. The interaction of trainer and trainee in seminars has many advantages. Theoretical knowledge is tested in practical exercises, such as announcing decisions or dealing with contempt. Tutors jointly plan a course, structure discussion and usually summarise the training course.

Sentencing exercises are particularly valued by chairmen and their colleagues. The form they take should reflect the training points covered by the course. The exemplary bench, consisting of judge, stipendiary magistrate and justice, against whose decisions those of the course members, divided into benches considering the same cases, may be discussed, offers great possibilities. Moreover, it helps bridge the gap between magistrates' courts and the Crown Courts. Sentencing exercises based on offences which can be tried either way must surely help to achieve a consensus on the principles of sentencing irrespective of the court. The sentencing exercise may be made more pertinent (and enjoyable) by role play and simulation.

Resources

Visual aids can be useful in training. They include the flip chart, the overhead projector, and video tapes. Prepared overhead projector transparencies with overlays can provide useful summaries of salient points. Prepared video tapes are expensive and they date. However, video recordings of practical exercises can be replayed for constructive comment.

The printed word is still an indispensable resource. Book lists are not an addendum to a course but an integral part of it. Their use is enhanced if reference books and text books are differentiated and important works or passages highlighted. The chairman should ensure that the magistrates' library is kept up to date. Journals are important. The Book List published every two years in *The Magistrate* is a helpful guide to relevant reading.

Administration

Magistrates are in part responsible for arranging their own training. Every chairman who is a member of a Magistrates' Courts Committee shares this role through its training sub-committee and the training officer whom the Courts Committee appoints. Maximum co-operation between training agencies should be encouraged. A variety of local patterns has emerged. Commonly there is an exchange of representatives as between the Magistrates' Association Branch executive or training sub-committee and the training sub-committee of the Magistrates' Courts Committee. This exchange avoids duplication and promotes programmes which dovetail into each other.

Partnership can produce jointly run courses, of which the administration is shared. The subject, content and agenda of each course needs to be carefully planned to make the best use of the time and space available. Receptivity can be facilitated by graduating the activities of the day from the more to the less demanding and by interspersing a variety of teaching methods.

CONCLUSION

Preparatory training is becoming more necessary and inevitable in many walks of life. The magistracy faces a particular challenge in meeting the demands of training. Justices come from many different backgrounds and experience. They have nevertheless to acquire a shared perception of the overriding claims of justice. The social exchange facilitated by training courses and less formal contact assists the development of this shared perception. Magistrates are unlikely to achieve as homogeneous an approach to their task as do those in the professions, who have to undergo much longer training. Some see this as a weakness, and others a strength since the bench reflects a whole range of social attitudes in the community.

Training which strengthens their corporate sense is designed to make justices better able to serve the community without creating a gap between them and the ordinary citizen. Magistrates do not have the popularly conceived remoteness of the higher judiciary. They must strike a balance between detachment from and identity with their peers.

Training is a key to the future proficiency of the magistracy. By training, the knowledge, expertise and experience of magistrates is passed on to tomorrow's chairmen and their fellow justices.

Chapter 8

Choosing chairmen

Suitability, not seniority, should be the first consideration in choosing chairmen. Experience is important, but it is not sufficient if other necessary qualities are lacking. No one should feel that long service brings with it an entitlement to preside: nor should anyone feel slighted if someone junior is chosen.

There are specific Rules[1] covering the annual election of a chairman and deputy chairman or chairmen of a bench. As to the choice of a person to preside over a court in the absence of the bench chairman or a deputy chairman, the Rules simply say that this may be made by any method which has been customary.

THE BENCH CHAIRMAN

Bench chairman is an office of considerable importance. Recognising this, the Lord Chancellor's Department has introduced a programme of training specifically for the chairman of each bench. It covers such subjects as the management of the bench, relationships with the clerk, the Advisory Committee, the Magistrates' Courts Committee, the deputy chairmen, the media and outside agencies generally. The list reflects the challenging task faced by bench chairmen.

Annual election meeting in October

The Rules provide for the annual election of a bench chairman at a meeting of the bench held in October. At least seven days' notice of the meeting must be given to each justice for the petty sessions area.

1 Justices of the Peace (Size and Chairmanship of Bench) Rules 1986, SI 1986/923.

No nominations and a secret ballot

No system of nominations is provided for and the election is by secret ballot. There is to be no disclosure of the way any magistrate has voted. Two alternative methods of balloting are prescribed (rule (5)). The chairman for the time being will give directions as to which of these procedures will be followed. He should reflect the views of the bench in his decision.

Different bench practices

Some benches have found the procedure in the Rules to be minimal and have evolved their own procedures appropriate to local circumstances. In the vast majority of cases there is no objection to these additional local arrangements, if they are obviously within the spirit of the Rules. Other practices are more dubious. A few examples may assist.

A secret ballot is clearly essential. Any other method, such as the passing of a resolution or arriving at a decision by general agreement, would not be within the Rules and the decision would be invalid. It has sometimes been felt that a system of nominations would be helpful, particularly to large benches. Accordingly, the Magistrates' Association suggested to the Lord Chancellor's Department in 1984 that benches should have the option of adopting a system providing for nominations. This did not meet with official favour. It was feared that if nominations were permitted there would be a risk of political interference in bench elections, with the main political parties ensuring that there were candidates from their ranks. Such interference would be most regrettable. Fortunately most bench elections take place without a hint of political manoeuvring. Indeed, it would be the duty of any magistrate approached on party political grounds to express strong disapproval of the approach.

Any arrangements by a bench to achieve nominations would not have the approval of the Lord Chancellor. However, there would seem to be no objection to a person who might attract the support of his colleagues indicating, if such is the case, that he does not wish to be elected. This avoids a situation in which a person is elected but declines to serve. Moreover, it prevents wasted votes and distortion of the voting in respect of persons willing to serve.

It is increasingly common for benches to adopt a convention placing a limit on the number of consecutive years a person may hold the office of bench chairman. In a way it is curious that a bench should feel the need to do this as the Rules provide for maximum flexibility by an annual opportunity to make a change. In practice, some benches have been reluctant to do so without the support of a convention of a limited period for holding office. The usual limit is a maximum term of three or five years. (There are a few benches which change their chairman every year. An annual change tends to make the office of bench chairman primarily honorific and militates against continuity of approach and policy.) This practice has now received official recognition and the Rules have been amended[2] to provide for a maximum number of five consecutive years of office as bench chairman subject to a proviso which would permit a bench to extend the term for good reason. For example, it may be that on a small bench there are only a few people with the necessary qualities and some of these may not wish to serve. Such a bench may pass a resolution in advance of the Annual Meeting that the normal Rule limiting the chairman's term of office shall not apply.

Who may vote?

Any justice who ordinarily acts in and for the petty sessions area may vote. This excludes anyone whose name has been placed on the Supplemental List. A newly appointed magistrate may not vote at an election held within the twelve months following his appointment but, rather curiously, other magistrates may vote for him, as his name will appear on the ballot list.

Two alternative methods of balloting

The traditional method of balloting, which was the only method until 1 October 1978, is for the clerk to prepare a ballot paper containing the names of all the members of the bench (other than those whose names have been entered on the Supplemental List) in alphabetical order. He will distribute these papers at the election meeting. A magistrate votes by placing a mark against the name of the person on the list whom he wishes to be chairman.

The second method was introduced primarily with larger benches in mind. It prevents a magistrate being faced for the first time at the election meeting with a formidably long list of names, many of which he probably does not recognise. The clerk prepares the same kind of alphabetical list as under the other method, but in this case sends each member of the bench a copy of the list with the notice of the meeting. Then at the meeting the clerk will hand each voting magistrate a ballot paper simply bearing the word 'Chairman'. A

2 Justices of the Peace (Size and Chairmanship of Bench) Rules 1986, SI 1986/923.

vote is recorded by writing on the paper the name of the magistrate the person voting wishes to be chairman.

Under each method the clerk collects the list or papers and counts the votes. A person will be elected on this ballot if he obtains more than half of the votes cast. If this occurs the clerk will announce the result, but if it does not there must be another ballot.

Before this is held the clerk will announce that no magistrate has obtained the requisite number of votes and will give the names of the magistrates for whom votes have been cast and the number of votes each of them has received. He will then distribute the lists or papers as on the first ballot and after the votes have been cast he will collect the papers and count the votes. If on this occasion a magistrate has obtained the required number of votes, the clerk will announce the result, otherwise there will be a third ballot conducted in the same manner as the other two ballots. If the result is conclusive the clerk will announce it, but this time, if the result is inconclusive, there will be no further ballot. Instead, the number of votes cast for each magistrate in the three ballots will be aggregated and the magistrate who has received the largest total of votes will be declared by the clerk to be the chairman.

On rare occasions, there is a tied result. If two or more magistrates have the same number of votes but have received more votes than any other magistrate, the clerk has to draw lots to decide which of them will be chairman. There is no definition in the Rules of *lot*; any convenient method is acceptable. The fact that headwear is not as fashionable as in former times is not likely to cause too much of a problem. The magistrate on whom the lot falls will be declared by the clerk to have been elected chairman. The election of deputy chairmen is dealt with later. A member of the clerk's staff may assist him in conducting the ballots, but he may not be assisted by one of the magistrates.

THE BENCH DEPUTY CHAIRMAN OR CHAIRMEN

This election may not take place until after the election of the bench chairman. The bench must first decide how many deputy chairmen it wishes to appoint. Some benches elect only one deputy chairman. This has some advantages as it makes clear who will deputise in the chairman's absence. Some benches elect enough deputy chairmen to ensure that every court that sits in the petty sessional division is presided over by an elected deputy chairman. This arrangement is often unpopular with the remaining members of the bench because it can limit opportunities for others to preside. The practice of most benches probably falls somewhere between these two extremes.

The ballot

The ballot is conducted in the same way as the ballot to elect the chairman. The name of the person elected chairman will be deleted from the ballot list. The clerk will distribute the ballot papers or ballot lists. On the first ballot it is a first-past-the-post system which determines the result. If there are two deputy chairmen to be elected, the two magistrates with the most votes will be elected, and so on. Again a tie may complicate matters. For example, if two deputy chairmen are to be elected, the fact that the two magistrates who are top of the poll receive the same number of votes will not matter as they will have obtained more votes than anyone else, but if the top three receive the same number of votes, or numbers two and three in the poll receive the same number of votes, there will have to be a second ballot. In the latter case, number one in the poll will be declared elected and the second ballot will be to elect the other deputy chairman. The clerk will announce that the ballot has been inconclusive, state the number of votes cast for each magistrate, and distribute another set of ballot papers. The name of any person elected on the first ballot will be deleted from the list. Papers will be marked 'Deputy Chairman – Second Ballot'. If on the second ballot one magistrate has most votes, he will be declared as the other deputy chairman. If the ballot is inconclusive, there will be no third ballot as in the election for bench chairman, neither will the votes be aggregated. The tie will be resolved by the clerk drawing lots.

CHAIRMAN FOR THE DAY

Few matters can arouse the members of a bench as easily as unsatisfactory arrangements for deciding who is to preside over a court in the absence of the bench chairman or a deputy chairman. It is essential for a bench to have a fixed procedure for making this decision.

Several methods are adopted by benches. It is not possible to say that one is to be preferred to another, because benches vary considerably in size and other characteristics. The main methods are:

By seniority

This was probably the usual way for benches to decide in the past. It is now widely recognised that this is not the most desirable system. Not only is it unlikely to ensure that the most suitable magistrates take the chair but it also causes frustration and resentment if it is apparent that a more senior colleague is demonstrably ill-equipped for the task. The Rules say that the decision as to who should take the chair may be made by any method which has been customary. They do not say that this custom cannot be changed.

By justices composing the court

Another common system is for the decision to be made by the magistrates composing each court. This practice accords with rule 8 of the Justices of the Peace (Size and Chairmanship of the Bench) Rules 1986. This can work well and can ensure that the magistrate presiding has the support of his colleagues. Sometimes, though, the very ad hoc nature of the method causes tensions and leads to demands for a more structured system with the decision made in advance.

Predetermination within the rota system

Many different rota systems operate. Some are based on magistrates attending on a particular day each week, or for a period of, say, a week or a month at regular intervals. Others draw up a rota for a quarter or even the whole year, with magistrates assigned to each court due to sit. Sometimes, even under a rota system, the decision as to who presides in court is left to be determined by the three magistrates assigned to each court or by the chairman or a deputy chairman, if present on the day.

We favour a decision taken in advance, at any rate on larger benches. This would mean that the growing number of courts which need to be serviced each day could be nucleated around chairmen designated in advance. If the rota is based on a day-of-the-week system, for example, the magistrates on the Monday rota may decide to appoint certain of their number to preside as needed. Although this is not provided for in the Rules, it would seem to be a system well within the discretion of a bench.

Perhaps what has been illustrated better than anything else is that there are many good and effective methods of selecting the right people as chairmen. Ultimately the policy that is adopted may be dictated by such matters as the size and number of retiring rooms in use by the bench, and whether all the justices sitting on a particular day are able to meet together in one retiring room or whether the groups of three justices meet in separate retiring rooms some distance from each other. Most obviously the size of the bench will be a very influential factor, and a system that works for a bench of a dozen members will not work for a bench of hundreds. What ultimately matters is that a bench can feel confident that it is choosing the most suitable people to be chairmen.

Chapter 9

The chairman of the bench

The judicial role of the bench is always central. However, the increasing size of benches, the growing complexity of their task, and the need of their colleagues for guidance and training, have increased the importance of all facets of the chairman's role. Many of his functions require special preparation. This is most helpfully given in Bench Chairmanship courses held at Madingley Hall, Cambridge, annually since December 1985. These courses assist bench chairmen to be fully appraised of the demands upon them on assuming office on the following 1 January and enable them to respond to them with greater confidence.

A bench chairman's main responsibilities as an efficient leader of his bench relate to:

HIS COLLEAGUE JUSTICES

They involve:

(a) The encouragement and support of newly appointed magistrates, not least by participation in their training both informal and formal.
(b) Ensuring that all magistrates keep abreast of legislation, procedure and judicial issues by regular attendance at training sessions provided by the bench, the Magistrates' Courts Committee and The Magistrates' Association. The provision and oversight of a bench library of books and journals, for which a colleague justice is responsible as librarian, can be invaluable.
(c) Being accessible to advise all colleagues who may have personal problems in the concept or discharge of their duties.

(d) Monitoring the conduct and competence of magistrates. Often intervention at an early stage of any difficulty can ensure that a potentially admirable justice is not lost to the bench.

RELATIONSHIP WITH THE CLERK

Organisational and administrative responsibilities:

(a) Convening and conducting bench meetings.
(b) Ensuring that rota and attendance arrangements accord with the interest of the bench at large: that all magistrates do a fair share of sittings, having regard to bench requirements and individual circumstances:
(c) Investigating high and low attendances.

RELATIONSHIP WITH ADVISORY COMMITTEES

RELATIONSHIP WITH THE LORD CHANCELLOR'S DEPARTMENT AND THE HOME OFFICE, AND MAGISTRATES' COURTS COMMITTEES

RELATIONS WITH OTHER AGENCIES IN THE PENAL AND JUDICIAL SPHERE

Insight into the work of the police, the prison service, the probation service and solicitors, always recognising the separate and independent role of each.

RELATIONSHIPS WITH THE MEDIA AND THE PUBLIC

(a) Guidance to other members of the bench.
(b) Attitudes to and handling of complaints.
(c) Relationships with particular groups, such as Members of Parliament.

Relationship with colleagues

The number of deputy chairmen varies from bench to bench, from one to a dozen or more. The mutual support and understanding between the chairman and deputy chairmen is one of the strengths of the bench. This does not just happen, especially when there is more than one deputy. The chairman will find it helpful to make definite and regular arrangements to meet his deputies, whether around the lunch or the committee room table. Here, among much else, agendas for bench meetings can be settled. Ultimate responsibility is with the chairman. Nevertheless, bench cohesion is fostered when decisions, participated in by deputy chairmen, are put into effect among colleagues with their help.

Definition of roles is desirable. This occurs naturally when a rota chairman has specific responsibility on his day. Where this is not the case, it may be useful to assign particular tasks to deputies on a regular basis or as they arise; for example, leading a discussion on a particular point, such as sentencing norms, at a bench meeting.

Chairmen and their deputies are experienced justices. They should bear in mind the perplexities of those in their formative months on the bench.

Now that the increasing size of benches can make even acquaintance between members difficult, the chairman should provide informal opportunities for meeting together. These may vary from a dinner to a cup of coffee before a bench meeting. Such events encourage the chairman in the proper art of delegation. A social committee brings responsibility to more magistrates and underlines the importance of individual participation in bench affairs.

Relationship with the clerk

Consultation between the chairman and the clerk should be regular, and cordiality its keynote. Full and frank discussion between them is vital to the efficiency and harmony of the bench. Their separate roles, however, should be as clear in the office as in court.

The staff, by statute, work under the direction of the clerk to the justices and are answerable to him. Official contact with them out of court should only be at the request of the clerk or with his agreement. The list of expectations from the staff is justifiably long. If colleagues feel that efficiency, courtesy, punctuality, sensitivity or legal expertise are deficient, it is for the chairman to grasp the nettle and raise the matter with the clerk. He should be equally eager to pass on commendation through the clerk, or by circulating a 'round robin' to staff with his consent. The clerk to the justices should deal with any complaints from the staff about magistrates, through the chairman.

Going through the agenda with the clerk before a bench meeting ensures consensus. It is in such a meeting that the relationship between the chairman and the clerk becomes an example to the whole bench. It is helpful to invite court clerks to attend justices' meetings so that all know how problems are resolved, as well as benefiting from informal discussions. Court clerks may in due course rise to higher office. The opportunity to meet with and discuss matters with magistrates will help them to become competent deputy clerks and later clerks to justices.

Organisational and administrative responsibilities

Administration is intended to enable any system, including the judicial, to fulfil its purpose by using its resources effectively and constructively. The chairman's conduct of a bench meeting is a sensitive indicator of his grasp of this fact.

Skill in the conduct of bench meetings, including handling multiple amendments without faltering, comes from careful preparation and growing experience. The bench meeting is a forum for the discussion of bench organisation. Organisational matters should not exclude consideration of the judicial function of the bench. Priority should be given to such matters as achieving consensus on the principles of sentencing in the light of new legislation, guidance from the High Court, and the requirement of consistency on the bench in question, having regard to area and national trends. Passing sentence is central to the magistrates' function. The Magistrates' Association tries to keep in step with bench and Branch opinion by, for example, close consultation in the formulation of its *Suggestions for Road Traffic Offence Penalties,* and frequent contributions to *The Magistrate* on sentencing.

The Advisory Committee system

As detailed descriptions of the Advisory System are available,[1] we include only a summary. The Advisory Committees are charged with finding suitable candidates for appointment to the Bench and recommending them to the Lord Chancellor (or the Chancellor of the Duchy of Lancaster); ensuring that justices fulfil their obligations; reviewing the situation annually and reporting it to the Lord Chancellor or the Duchy Chancellor. There are 96 Advisory Committees, one for each London Commission area, one for each non-metropolitan county, and one or more for each metropolitan district. In addition, certain large urban areas in some non-metropolitan counties have their own Advisory Committees. Most

1 'The Appointment of Justices of the Peace' (1984) 40 The Magistrate at p 69.

of the non-metropolitan county Advisory Committees have sub-committees, sometimes known as Area Panels. These total 147.

The Chancellor of the Duchy of Lancaster acts in the counties of Greater Manchester, Merseyside and Lancashire. In the City of London, the Lord Mayor and Aldermen continue to be justices ex officio and sit alongside appointed justices. In both areas the Advisory Committee system works in the same way as in the rest of the country in most respects. All appointments to Advisory Committees and sub-committees are made by the Lord Chancellor or Duchy Chancellor personally. It is usual for the Lord Lieutenant to be appointed chairman of the Advisory Committee in a non-metropolitan county. Most Advisory Committees have 8 to 10 members. Sub-committees tend to be rather smaller. The normal period of appointment is six years, with half the Committee or sub-committee retiring every three years. Most members are magistrates; only about 8% have not served as such. It is made clear that each is appointed in a personal capacity and not as a representative.

Party politics have no part in the system, although Lord Chancellors have laid great emphasis upon achieving a political balance on committees. Committees receive directions and guidance from the Lord Chancellor, but within this framework they have wide discretion in the way they conduct their business. The Lord Chancellor has emphasised the importance of candidates being interviewed, while allowing local discretion as to the number and location of interviews. The main purposes of the interview are to establish whether the candidate has judicial potential, understands what is involved in becoming a justice of the peace, and is able to meet the commitment.

Frequently, in the media, the 'secrecy' of the system is criticised. It is true that only two Advisory Committees, those for Inner London and Essex, publish the names of their members.[2] The usual reason advanced for this is to protect members from being lobbied.[3] It is also true that proceedings of Committees are necessarily confidential. However, the name of the secretary to the Advisory Committee (42 Advisory Committees and 97 sub-committees have a justices' clerk as secretary) is publicised locally.

It is common nowadays for notices to be placed in newspapers, and for approaches to be made to local organisations, drawing

2 The Lord Chancellor leaves this to individual Advisory Committees to decide. He has recently given approval to the North East London Area Advisory Committee disclosing its membership.

3 Mr Brian Cooke JP, Secretary of Commissions, and Sir Thomas Skyrme JP *The Changing Image of the Magistracy*, 2nd edn, p 48.

attention to the need for candidates. Considerable efforts are made to attract candidates from all sections of the community, and the fact that these have not always been successful has not been for the want of trying, as Sir Thomas Skyrme explains in his book.[4]

Some Advisory Committees have experienced great difficulty in attracting suitable candidates to achieve the necessary balance on benches in their area. Undoubtedly economic constraints have exacerbated these difficulties. Many employers are more reluctant than in the past to underwrite time off for public duties. Section 29 of the Employment Protection (Consolidation) Act 1978 requires an employer to permit an employee who is a magistrate to take time off to attend court, but the amount of time that may be taken must be reasonable, taking into account the circumstances of the employer's business and the effect of the absence on the running of that business.

Increasingly magistrates are finding themselves under pressure from employers to reduce the number of days they serve. One effect of this, and other similar pressures, is that a number of magistrates appointed to any bench will only be able to undertake the minimum number of attendances required. Therefore the size of the bench has to increase if other magistrates are not to be required to undertake an undesirably high number of attendances.

What level of attendances is considered to be too high? Some argue that a fair share is within a reasonable margin of the average attendance of the bench as a whole.[5] It is generally accepted that a reasonable maximum would be between 50 and 60 attendances per year. Chairmen and deputy chairmen may well sit up to 70 to 80 times. If a bench's annual return of attendances discloses that any magistrate has attended on more than 100 occasions, a letter is sent to the Advisory Committee by the Lord Chancellor's Department pointing out that this is regarded as excessive.

A delicate balance has to be maintained. In order to recruit as wide a cross-section of magistrates as possible, it may be necessary to accept a number who can only offer the minimum of 26 half-day attendances. This means an increased load on others. An individual magistrate's work load should not be so great as to risk the necessity of appointing two or three new justices to replace him on retirement.

Conduct

Perhaps the relationship of a chairman of a bench with the Advisory

4 *The Changing Image of the Magistracy,* 2nd edn, chs 4 and 5, pp 36-67.
5 'Fair Shares' (1984) 40 The Magistrate at p 66.

Committee can best be illustrated by an example. Assume that a complaint is made about a magistrate's conduct. What should the chairman do?

If the complaint seems to be one which the chairman can properly handle himself, he should first establish the facts. He should arrange to meet the magistrate privately, in appropriate cases with the clerk to the justices in attendance. The substance of the complaint should be put to the magistrate and he should be given ample opportunity to respond. If it is felt necessary to give any advice, a written record of it should be kept. A report of the interview should be forwarded to the Advisory Committee for information.

If there are a series of complaints, or a complaint which the chairman feels would more appropriately be dealt with by the Advisory Committee, the chairman, or the clerk on his behalf, should refer the matter to the Advisory Committee. The chairman of the Committee will decide if it is necessary for the magistrate to be seen by an interviewing panel. If so, the secretary will normally specify the nature of the complaint to the magistrate in writing in advance of the interview. The panel will give the magistrate a full opportunity to answer the complaint. They will forward a report of the interview to the Advisory Committee. If further action is considered necessary, the Committee will forward their recommendation to the Lord Chancellor.

Occasionally a chairman will come across cases where it would be wise to seek the advice of the Advisory Committee before any action is taken. If necessary, the Advisory Committee will refer the matter to the Lord Chancellor at that stage.

The role of the Home Office and the Lord Chancellor's Department

There is a division of responsibility between the Lord Chancellor's Department and the Home Office in relation to the magistrates' courts system in England and Wales.

Both the Lord Chancellor and the Home Secretary are, of course, senior members of the Cabinet. The primary role of the Lord Chancellor in relation to the magistracy is that of Head of the Judiciary. He sees the maintenance of the independence and quality of the judiciary as his most important responsibility.

The Home Secretary has responsibilities for the maintenance of the Queen's Peace, exercised through the police, probation and prison services; criminal justice policy and criminal justice legislation; advice through Home Office circulars; decisions on appeals by local authorities against policy decisions made by Magistrates' Courts Committees (p 92); changes in petty sessional division boundaries; appointment of justices' clerks; staff training; the qualification of court clerks; and – anachronistically – justices' allowances.

In 1985-6, the Home Office spent £165 million on magistrates' courts. Decisions on expenditure are made locally through Magistrates' Courts Committees. Understandably, the Home Office has recently sought to ensure that value for money is given by obtaining management information and performance indicators from magistrates' courts.

Management and efficiency have become bywords. Efficiency is a desirable and worthwhile aim, but it is not an end in itself. Administrative decisions can influence the quality of justice dispensed and this is paramount. Administrative convenience may, for example, suggest a certain policy on remand procedures or fine enforcement, but a chairman must be careful to ensure that this policy is also in the interests of justice.

A series of recent cases have given warning of this.[6] The High Court has ruled that where magistrates have suspended on terms a warrant of commitment for default in paying a sum, the warrant may not be issued without a judicial hearing. With hindsight it may seem obvious that this is only natural justice, but until recently it was the general practice of magistrates' courts to issue such warrants without notice, such being the administratively cheaper and more convenient course.

Apart from his role as a senior member of the Cabinet and Head of the Judiciary, the Lord Chancellor is Speaker of the House of Lords and Ministerial head of a large Department of State with 10,000 staff. His responsibilities include legal and certain ecclesiastical appointments, the appointment of Queen's Counsel; law reform; administration of courts (apart from magistrates' courts) and tribunals; legal aid; and he is the responsible Minister for the Public Trustee, Official Solicitor, Public Record Office, Land Registry and the Law Commission.

He appoints justices of the peace on the advice of his local Advisory Committees, and is responsible for their effectiveness and conduct. He is responsible for policy on the training of magistrates through the Judicial Studies Board (previously the Advisory Committee on the Training of Magistrates – the Boreham Committee) and his Training Officer. He specifies the training required. He approves schemes of instruction devised by Magistrates' Courts Committees. He approves training provided by

6 *Re Forrest* [1981] AC 1038, *Wilson v Colchester Justices* [1985] 2 All ER 97.

the Magistrates' Association and certain other bodies such as universities.

Of these roles, the one with which a new chairman will need to be familiar is that concerning the appointment and removal of magistrates. Some of the most difficult decisions he will face will be those relating to the conduct and performance of his colleagues.

The role of the Magistrates' Courts Committee

The Magistrates' Courts Committee is composed in accordance with the Magistrates' Courts Committees (Constitution) Regulations 1973. In non-metropolitan counties and metropolitan districts not divided into petty sessional divisions, the Committee numbers between 6 and 18 members. Elsewhere, the size depends on the numbers of members each petty sessional division may appoint at the October meeting (ie number of members on bench divided by 20 – if a whole number is not obtained, the next largest whole number. If this produces more than 35 members on the Committee, the formula is adjusted.) Members hold office from 1 December for one year and are eligible for re-appointment. In metropolitan districts, the justices' clerk is ex officio clerk of the committee. In non-metropolitan districts, other persons may be appointed, but the majority of Committees have appointed justices' clerks.

The responsibilities of a Committee are set out in the Justices of the Peace Act 1979, section 19 et seq, and include the division of a non-metropolitan county into petty sessional areas; the provision of training courses for justices; the appointment of clerks to the justices and their staffs; determining what provision should be made in the way of courthouses and equipment; authorising costs incurred by justices. Magistrates' Courts Committees have no involvement in matters relating to the judicial functioning of the courts.

A Committee may at any time submit proposals to the Home Secretary for alteration of divisions. Before making proposals, the Committee must consult the local authorities and the justices concerned. The Home Secretary may direct a Committee to carry out a review, and may carry out the review himself if the Committee fails to act within six months.

The Committee may act through sub-committees. It is common for a training sub-committee to be appointed to make provision for courses of instruction for justices. All Committees now appoint a training officer. Any scheme devised must be in accordance with arrangements approved by the Lord Chancellor. If a Committee fails to carry out this task, the Lord Chancellor may step in and provide the training and recover the cost from the Courts Committee. To avoid duplication, it is important that there should be adequate liaison between the Committee, the local branch or branches of The Magistrates' Association and other agencies involved in training, such as universities and other educational establishments. Stage I training of new magistrates is very often delegated by the Committee to the local bench. A new chairman should discuss their respective roles in training with the clerk to the justices.

The appointment of clerks to justices and their staff, staff establishments, gradings and the like, are vital though time-consuming responsibilities of the Committee. There is an interesting difference between the relationship of a clerk to the justices to the Committee and that of the rest of the staff. A clerk holds office during the pleasure of the Committee, but he is not employed by the Committee: the rest of the staff are. Neither is the clerk an employee of the magistrates he serves. His accountability is a matter of some complexity. The clerk holds a statutory appointment. He is personally responsible for the discharge of his functions and for the management of his office. Nevertheless, his justices exercise an independent judicial role, and the clerk, as their legal adviser, must be free to tender the advice which he feels is right, whether it pleases the Courts Committee or his justices or not. A clerk to the justices is appointed by the Committee and the appointment is subject to the approval of the Home Secretary. He may be dismissed by the Committee at any time, but the magistrates for the division or divisons he serves must first be consulted. If they do not agree that the clerk should be dismissed, the Committee must seek the Home Secretary's approval for their decision.

It is the duty of the Committee to provide a clerk with the necessary staff to carry out his tasks. National conditions of service are negotiated by the Joint Negotiating Committee for Justices' Clerks' Assistants. All posts are graded. Each Committee reviews staff arrangements periodically, usually annually. A chairman will be wise not to become involved in staff matters at bench level unless requested to do so by the clerk. If magistrates have complaints about a particular member of staff, say a court clerk, the chairman should discuss this with the clerk to the justices in the first instance. Only if the matter cannot be resolved between them should it go to the Courts Committee for decision. It is quite usual for a Committee to delegate to the clerk the appointment of staff in the lower grades, and since 1 October 1980 Committees have been responsible for deciding whether to grant certificates of competence to individual court clerks who do not hold a legal or other requisite qualification.

After consultation with the local authority, the Committee must decide what provision is to be made for courthouses, furniture, books and equipment in its area. There has been criticism in the past that too many Committees have acted as if they were sub-committees of the local authority and have been subservient to the views of the authority. A Magistates' Courts Committee is a distinct legal entity and is quite separate from the local authority. The Committee is bound to consult the local authority on certain matters, but it is the Committee that must make the determinations. If the local authority feels aggrieved by determinations of the Courts Committee, it may appeal to the Home Secretary. Of any expenditure by local authorities on magistrates' courts, a grant of 80% will be received from central government, so that only 20% will fall on the local ratepayers.

The Magistrates' Courts Committee is responsible for decisions which can assist or hinder the work of the bench. Some benches do not ensure appropriate representation on these Committees and some chairmen give too little opportunity for the discussion of appropriate Magistrates' Courts Committee business at bench meetings. Qualification for membership of the Committee, and whether or not the chairman of the bench should be a member, are aspects of the Committee too rarely discussed by magistrates. Bench chairmen should remedy the situation.

Relations with other agencies

Many benches now have court users groups, chaired by the clerk, the chairman, or another senior magistrate. Whether or not there is such a group, the chairman should ensure that a bench has some arrangements for liaison with the police, the probation service, solicitors and others who use the court. The introduction of the Crown Prosecution Service has led to suggestions that prosecuting solicitors will in future be seeking to organise court sittings and other arrangements to their own convenience. This is a clear example of a situation calling for liaison and co-operation. Individual services cannot take independent action, ignoring the effect this will have on the other agencies. Some apparently small change, such as the time a court starts or finishes, may have considerable implications for others.

By statute, magistrates largely compose the Probation Area Committees which are responsible for the direction of the probation service. The day-to-day management is in the hands of the chief probation officer and his senior staff and is in line with the policy of the Probation Area Committee. Probation Liaison Committees are a forum for the exchange of views in an area vital to sentencing. Even if the bench chairman is not a member of either of these Committees, the effectiveness of both is influenced by the insights of the bench. Here the chairman ought to be a vital link.

The media

Public order issues, industrial action, Christmas drink/drive campaigns, and like matters, bring magistrates courts into the media limelight. If an inquiry from the media concerns a particular case, no comment is the wise course. It will be more appropriate for the Lord Chancellor's Department or the Magistrates' Association to deal with this kind of inquiry, and even then only in general terms.

But there are matters on which it may be sensible for the chairman to comment. For example, if there has been inaccurate reporting or some clarification is necessary. This happened recently when a bench was criticised for leniency when binding over a football hooligan who went on to the pitch and interfered with the referee. It had not been understood that that was the only course open to the bench as the police had brought the matter before the court on a complaint requesting a binding over rather than charging the defendant with an offence. Either the chairman or clerk to the justices could make the explanation to the press in such an instance. If a statement is on behalf of the justices, it should generally be made by the chairman. If it is a technical or procedural point, the chairman may request the clerk to deal with the matter.

It helps if good relations are built up with the local press and radio station. If there is mutual confidence, few difficulties will arise. The national press, radio and television pose different problems. Any issue which could attract wider public interest could become an item of national news. Local reporters may pass on stories to national newspapers and programmes.

The chairman of the bench should ensure that colleagues are aware of the hazards of making statements to reporters and the need to contact the chairman or clerk to the justices if they are approached to do so. If the chairman is unsure of the course to take, he should consult with the clerk, who may advise him to contact the Advisory Committee, the Lord Chancellor's Department or the Magistrates' Association. It can be a chastening experience to find an off-the-cuff remark reported on the front page of a national newspaper! Safeguards here, as in all judicial duties, lie in ready access to the advice of the clerk, in training and in experience.

The chairman and his colleagues, the clerk and his staff, are linked in partnership. On the strength of this link rests the quality of justice in magistrates' courts.

Appendices

APPENDIX I

The lay justices and the clerk in the magistrates' court

Summary of existing position in law and good practice
A statement agreed by the Association with the Justices' Clerks' Society

Constitution of magistrates' court

1. A bench of lay justices is, in law, competent to constitute a magistrates' court and to discharge its functions without the presence of a clerk.

In practice a court would not and could not work without a clerk. It is his presence and participation, complementing that of the justices, that makes it a fully competent court of law capable of dealing with the wide range of cases within its jurisdiction. The proper relationship, of which a complete definition has never been attempted, between the bench and the clerk needs not only to be understood and given practical effect by them but also to be recognised and accepted by those who are concerned in the work of magistrates' courts.

2. A statement of the law on these matters will be found in *Stone's Justices' Manual,* 1974 edition, pp 4 to 6.[1]

Responsibilities of clerk

3. The clerk may properly assist the justices, where appropriate and necessary, as follows:
(1) by advising them on matters of law, practice and procedure;
(2) by directing their attention to the issues involved in a matter

1 Now *Stone's Justices' Manual,* 1987 edition, paras 1-2 to 1-29.

before the court and the respective burdens and standards of proof;

(3) by refreshing their memories as to any matter of evidence, eg by referring to any notes taken;

(4) as to the general level of sentences, as to their sentencing powers, and as to any consequential matters which may follow upon conviction.

The clerk must not be a party to findings of fact nor to the determination of a sentence to be imposed or an order to be made.

Conduct of proceedings

4. The extent to which the conduct of proceedings is to be regulated by the justices or by the clerk is essentially a matter for agreement between them. In all matters save the pronouncement of a decision of the court it is proper for the justices if they so wish to delegate the conduct of proceedings to the clerk so, however, that it is made manifest that the justices have overriding responsibility.

5. Within the sphere of his responsibilities, it is right for the clerk to assist the justices by intervening in the proceedings to raise any matter relevant to the issue before the court. Where the court is required or wishes to assist an unrepresented party, it is preferable that the action should be undertaken by the clerk.

Advice of the clerk

6. As a matter of good practice, justices should accept the clerk's advice on matters of law, practice and procedure, and they are entitled to expect him to give such advice. A distinction should, however, be drawn between circumstances where a binding statement of ascertained law can be made and those where no binding authority is known. Where authority exists the justices are entitled to be satisfied as to its existence and meaning, and the clerk must be prepared to refer the justices to the relevant provision or decision. The justices should in those circumstances follow the advice of the clerk. But where there is no binding authority it is the clerk's responsibility as between him and the justices to refer the justices to such law as is available, in so far as the parties have not already done so. He may further assist the justices by offering his opinion as to the most appropriate decision (in law), but the ultimate responsibility for deciding the matter is that of the justices.

Retirement

7. When the justices retire from the court for private consideration,

the clerk should not retire with them as a matter of course, but justices should not be discouraged from seeking his assistance either in open court or in their retiring room within the field in which he can legitimately advise them. Provided the clerk is discharging his legitimate functions it is not improper for him to remain with the justices throughout their retirement, but it is good practice for him to return to the court before the justices.

Justices' clerks' assistants

8. The justices' clerk remains responsible, as between the justices and himself, when the duties of Clerk at a court sitting are being carried out by someone on his behalf, but the justices are entitled to request the attendance and personal advice of the justices' clerk, on any question of law, practice or procedure arising in the proceedings. This right to the personal advice of the justices' clerk may be particularly valuable when the duties of court clerk are being performed by an assistant who has only a limited amount of experience or legal knowledge.

Adopted by the Council, 21 November 1974.

APPENDIX II

The role of the clerk in court

The terms of the 1981 *Practice Direction* ([1981] 2 All ER 831) about the role of the clerk in court are as follows—

'1. A justices' clerk is responsible to the justices for the performance of any of the functions set out below by any member of his staff acting as court clerk and may be called in to advise the justices even when he is not personally sitting with the justices as clerk to the court.

2. It shall be the resonsibility of the justices' clerk to advise the justices as follows—

(*a*) on questions of law or of mixed law and fact;
(*b*) as to matters of practice and procedure.

3. If it appears to him necessary to do so, or he is so requested by the justices, the justices' clerk has the responsibility to—

(*a*) refresh the justices' memory as to any matter of evidence and to draw attention to any issues involved in the matters before the court;

(*b*) advise the justices generally on the range of penalties which the law allows them to impose and on any guidance relevant to the choice of penalty provided by the law, the decisions of the superior courts or other authorities.

If no request for advice has been made by the justices, the justices' clerk shall discharge his responsibility in court in the presence of the parties.
4. The way in which the justices' clerk should perform his functions should be stated as follows—

(*a*) The justices are entitled to the advice of their clerk when they retire in order that the clerk may fulfil his responsibility outlined above.
(*b*) Some justices may prefer to take their own notes of evidence. There is, however, no obligation upon them to do so. Whether they do so or not, there is nothing to prevent them from enlisting the aid of their clerk and his notes if they are in any doubt as to the evidence which has been given.
(*c*) If the justices wish to consult their clerk solely about the evidence or his notes of it, this should ordinarily, and certainly in simple cases, be done in open court. The object is to avoid any suspicion that the clerk has been involved in deciding issues of fact.

5. For the reasons stated in the Practice Direction of 15 January 1954 ([1954] 1 All ER 230) which remains in full force and effect, in domestic proceedings it is more likely than not that the justices will wish to consult their clerk. In particular, where rules of court require the reasons for their decision to be drawn up in consultation with the clerk, they will need to receive his advice for this purpose.
6. This Practice Direction is issued with the concurrence of the President of the Family Division.'

APPENDIX III

General powers and duties of justices' clerks (Justices of the Peace Act 1979, s 28(3) and (4))

(3) It is hereby declared that the functions of a justices' clerk include the giving to the justices to whom he is clerk or any of them, at the request of the justices or justice, of advice about law, practice or procedure on questions arising in connection with the discharge of their or his functions, including questions arising when the clerk is not personally attending on the justices or justice, and that the

clerk may, at any time when he thinks he should do so, bring to the attention of the justices or justice any point of law, practice or procedure that is or may be involved in any question so arising.

In this subsection the reference to the functions of justices or a justice is a reference to any of their or his functions as justices or a justice of the peace, other than functions as a judge of the Crown Court.

(4) The enactment of subsection (3) above shall not be taken as defining or in any respect limiting the powers and duties belonging to a justices' clerk or the matters on which justices may obtain assistance from their clerk.

APPENDIX IV[1]

Structured decision-making

(1) THE HEARING OF NOT GUILTY CASES

Identification of accused
Charge
Plea
Prosecution outline
Prosecution evidence
Cross examination
Submission of no case to answer
Defence evidence
Cross-examination
Defence summing-up
Clerk's advice
Verdict
Antecedents
Costs and compensation
Sentence
Pronouncement
Terms of payment

(2) GUILTY OR NOT GUILTY

A structured discussion

What is the STANDARD OF PROOF required in this case? Beyond reasonable doubt? On a balance of probabilities?

1 This example is given because it includes the essential elements of a structure for structured decisions while recognising that the form of application for remand in custody/conditions of bail is now made by the Crown Prosecution Service rather than the police.

What is the LAW in this case? What are the legal elements of the offence? How many of those were in dispute?

What was the EVIDENCE in this case? What was agreed? What was in dispute?

How do we EVALUATE the disputed evidence? Whom do we believe? Is there independent support?

Can we now agree on a VERDICT?

Where are the REASONS for our verdict?

(3) THE SENTENCING DECISION

The offence. How serious is it? How much harm was done? How much gain was made?

Penalties. What is the maximum? What is the bench norm? Is there legal guidance?

The offender. What is the personal background, family situation, etc? What is his attitude to the offence? Are there mitigating factors? Do we need the help of SER's?

Sentencing objective. Is our primary objective to punish? Or to rehabilitate? Or to deter? Or to protect society?

Options. What options are open to the Bench? Can any be ruled out by the nature of the offence? Which option is most likely to secure our objective?

Custody. How short can it be? Is it possible to suspend it? Is it possible to suspend part of it?

Ancillary matters. Is he in breach of other sentences? Are costs appropriate? Can he be made to pay compensation?

Sentence. What is to be the sentence?

Reasons. What are our reasons?

Explanations. Are any explanations needed?

Check with the clerk

The pronouncement

A guideline of matters to be considered when deciding guilty or not guilty and sentence

Published by The Berkshire Branch of the Magistrates' Association

(1) A GUIDELINE OF MATTERS TO BE CONSIDERED WHEN DECIDING 'GUILTY' OR 'NOT GUILTY'

1. The charge

Justices should remind themselves of the full wording of the charge(s). It is good practice to ask the clerk to repeat it (and explain it if necessary) after hearing all the evidence.

2. (a) Burden of proof

Consider the burden of proof. Who has to prove what? Usually the Prosecution have to prove every part of the charge but occasionally there are matters which the defendant has to prove.

(b) Standard of proof

Consider the standard of proof. Usually the prosecution have to prove everything beyond reasonable doubt. If there are any matters which the defence have to prove the standard is on the balance of probabilities which means it is more likely than not.

3. Elements of the offence

Note (in writing if necessary) the elements which make up the offence. If in doubt about these consult the Clerk.

4. Legal defence

Consider whether there is any legal defence available to the defendant.

5. Establish the evidence

(a) What facts are agreed by the prosecution and defence.
(b) What facts are in dispute
- Weigh up the evidence on these from both sides.
- Whom do you believe? And Why?
- What do you believe?
- Discuss and agree these.

6. The decision

Put together all the facts that you find proved and match these to the elements of the offence.
- Are all the elements proved?
- If in doubt dismiss the charge.

7. Confirming the decision

The chairman may sum up briefly what is agreed on the evidence and the reasons for the decision.

(2) A GUIDELINE OF MATTERS TO BE CONSIDERED WHEN DECIDING SENTENCE

Consultation with the clerk

While the justices' clerk has no role in the actual determination of the sentence, *Practice Direction* [1981] 2 All ER 831 emphasises that he has responsibility 'either if it appears to him necessary to do so or he is so requested by the Justices to advise the Justices generally on the range of penalties which the law allows them to impose and on any guidance relevant to the choice of penalty provided by the law, the decisions of the superior courts or other authorities'.

1. The offence

(a) How serious is this type of offence in relation to all the offences dealt with by the court?
(b) Has your bench an agreed starting point for this type of offence?
(c) How serious is this offence of its type? or 'What has the defendant done?'
(d) Consider any aggravating factors, eg planned or deliberate nature of the offence, the victim (is it a child, elderly person, person in public office), use of violence, breach of trust, prevalence of offence, number of offences committed.
(e) Consider extenuating facts, eg the offence committed on sudden impulse, provocation, influence of other persons.

2. Offender

(a) Consider personal factors, eg age, income, family situation, health and employment.
(b) Consider defendant's previous convictions. Give less weight if they are thought different types of offence and if long time gaps.

3. The object of the sentence

- Decide what your sentence is aimed to achieve.
- Punish the offender?
- Deter the offender and others?

- Rehabilitate the offender?
- Compensate the victim?
- Protect the public?
- Prevention for the future?

4. Social Enquiry Report

Consider whether an SER is required by law. If not, consider whether it is necessary to have an SER and if so, why? What matters do you wish to be investigated? Suitability for CSO?

5. The sentence

(a) Consider the options available.

(1) *Defendant aged 17-21:* Probation Order; deferment of sentence; hospital order; absolute discharge; conditional discharge; fine and/or compensation; (attendance centre); community service order; Detention centre; Youth custody; Committal to Crown Court for sentence.

Consult the Clerk if you are considering a custodial sentence for a defendant aged between 17 and 20 years.

(2) *Defendants aged 21 or over:* Probation Order; deferment of sentence; hospital order; absolute discharge; conditional discharge; fine and/or compensation; community service order; suspended or partially suspended sentence of imprisonment; immediate imprisonment; committal to Crown Court for sentence.

(b) Legal Aid

If a custodial sentence is being considered consider whether the defendant should have an opportunity to be represented.

(c) Custodial sentence

(i) Is the court satisfied, considering the offence and the offender, that prison is necessary?
(ii) Can a CSO be used as an alternative?
(iii) Can the sentence be wholly or partially suspended?
(iv) If the offender has not served a prison sentence before, is the court satisfied that no other method of dealing with him is appropriate?
What are the court's reasons for being satisfied of this? Note: these have to be stated in Court.
(v) What is the shortest appropriate prison term? (in weeks)

(d) Fines

Consider the defendant's ability to pay. Fines should be fixed at such a level that the defendant may pay them off within a year. If a compensation order is made, then a slightly longer period is permissible.

(e) Ancillary matters

Bind over?
Is he in breach of other sentence or orders?
Costs? Disqualification, licence endorsed, penalty points?

6. The announcement of the sentence

Chairman to write down the agreed sentence and any agreed comments.

Justices should always be ready to check at this stage with the clerk.

APPENDIX V

A structure for bail decisions

PROCEDURE BEFORE A MAGISTRATES' COURT FOR BAIL OR CUSTODY

IDENTIFICATION
The Clerk identifies the defendant (if present), his solicitor, and puts the charges if necessary.

ADJOURNMENT?
The Court hears the application for an adjournment and gives it judicial consideration. If the adjournment is granted, the Clerk invites the prosecutor to make his application.

TYPE OF APPLICATION
The prosecutor says his application is

UNCONDITIONAL BAIL	CONDITIONAL BAIL	CUSTODY
No objection to unconditional bail.	No objection to bail, but conditions sought.	To withhold bail. NB (i) If second or subsequent bail appearance, are defence alleging a change of circumstances? (ii) Is it an application for a remand in absence?

DOES DEFENCE AGREE?

The Clerk asks if the defence agree to the application, and the defence indicates its position.

PROSECUTION APPLICATION

The Clerk asks the Prosecutor to make his application.
The Prosecutor makes his application as follows:–

UNCONDITIONAL BAIL	CONDITIONAL BAIL	CUSTODY
Facts of case (if requested by the Court or the defence). Previous convictions. T.I.C.s.	Facts of case. Grounds for conditions. Conditions sought. T.I.C.s. Previous convictions.	Facts of case. EXCEPTIONS (Bail Act) GROUNDS relied on to substantiate exceptions. Previous convictions. T.I.C.s.

DEFENCE APPLICATION

The Clerk asks the defence

UNCONDITIONAL BAIL	CONDITIONAL BAIL	CUSTODY
Are there any other comments?	Are the grounds for conditions accepted? Do you agree with the conditions? Are there any other comments?	Do you wish to address the Court on the question IF YES – Court hears the application in full (unless no change in circumstances, IF NO – Court must still be satisfied that EXCEPTIONS and REASONS exist.

RIGHTS OF REPLY

UNCONDITIONAL BAIL	CONDITIONAL BAIL	CUSTODY
Not applicable	Prosecution have the right of reply if the defence offer bail conditions or sureties not earlier notified to them. Discretion to allow further comments by defence.	Prosecution have the right of reply if defence are putting forward matters prosecution knows not correct.

COURT QUERIES

UNCONDITIONAL BAIL	CONDITIONAL BAIL	CUSTODY
Probably not applicable	Court to investigate the feasibility of conditions or suitability of sureties. Prosecution or Court can question sureties.	Court can investigate any ambiguities, calling for evidence if necessary.

DECISION

UNCONDITIONAL BAIL	CONDITIONAL BAIL	CUSTODY
Announce adjournment date and time. **WARN** about failure to attend.	**Announce** adjournment date and time. **Announce** GROUNDS for conditions. **Announce** CONDITIONS. **WARN** about (i) failure to attend. (ii) failure to abide by conditions.	**Announce** adjournment date and time. **Announce** EXCEPTIONS. **Announce** REASONS.

LEICESTERSHIRE CONSTABULARY*

APPLICATION FOR REMAND IN CUSTODY/CONDITIONAL BAIL

Your Worships,

In this matter the Police application is that the accused .... **be remanded:—**

☐ In Police custody
☐ In custody other than in Police custody.
☐ On conditional bail.
☐ Unruliness certificate applied for.

For .... days/until*...........

For the purpose of:—

☐ Preparation of the prosecution case.
☐ Preparation for committal proceedings.
☐ That he may be questioned about other matters.
☐ Further enquiries necessary in this case.
☐ Other reason? Details ....

*Although bail applications are now presented by the Crown Prosecutor, this form of application is included because it is thought still to be of value as a guide.

BRIEF facts of the case and circumstances of arrest (see precis)

The Police rely on the following exceptions to the right for bail:—

- ☐ Would fail to surrender.
- ☐ Would commit further offences.
- ☐ Would interfere with witnesses/obstruct the course of justice*.
- ☐ Impracticable to obtain sufficient information for a bail decision.
- ☐ Impracticable to obtain reports or complete enquiries for sentencing purposes.
- ☐ Custody being for his own protection/welfare*.
- ☐ Already serving a custodial sentence.
- ☐ Arrested for absconding/breaking conditions* of present bail. Details ....
- ☐ Previously broke conditions/failed to answer bail in criminal proceedings.

The Police put forward the following grounds in support of the exceptions previously listed:—

- ☐ Nature/gravity* of the offence – as previously described.
- ☐ Likelihood of a custodial sentence being imposed upon conviction.

(i) Previous convictions (agree with defence first)? Yes/No* (Read out)

(ii) T.I.C.s? Yes/No* (Summarise)

- ☐ Character/Associates/Lack of Community Ties*

(i)	Identity established?	Yes/No*
(ii)	Fixed abode?	Yes/No*
(iii)	If no fixed abode, how long?	________
(iv)	Has he wife/children?	Yes/No*
(v)	Does he live with them?	Yes/No*
(vi)	Does he support them?	Yes/No*
(vii)	Is he employed?	Yes/No*
(viii)	If employed, how long?	________
(ix)	Does he travel abroad?	Yes/No*
(x)	Is he one of several persons of the same area charged together?	Yes/No*
(xi)	Has he mental/physical* health problems?	Yes/No*

Details ____

____

- ☐ Present offence committed on bail.
- ☐ Details of previous occasions of offending on bail.

____

____

____

☐ Previous convictions (To be agreed with defence before reading out details)
(Separate list if necessary).

____

____

____

☐ Other relevant information.

____

____

____

Conditional Bail:

Conditions — The Prosecution seek the following conditions:

____

____

____

*Delete if inapplicable.

APPENDIX VI

Award of costs to defendants in criminal cases in the magistrates' courts (*Practice Note (Justices: Defendant's Costs)* [1982] 3 All ER 1152, per Lord Lane CJ)

1. I understand that there is a need for guidance to magistrates in exercising their powers to order costs in indictable offences.
2. Under section 1 of the Costs in Criminal Cases Act 1973 a magistrates' court dealing summarily with an indictable offence and dismissing the information, or inquiring into any offence as examining justices and determining not to commit the accused for trial, may order the payment out of central funds of the costs of the defence. A similar power exists under section 12(1) of the Act where an information is not proceeded with.
3. Whether to make such an award is a matter in the unfettered discretion of the court in the light of the circumstances of each particular case.
4. It should be accepted as normal practice that such an award be made unless there are positive reasons for making a different order. Examples of such reasons are:—
   (a) Where the prosecution has acted spitefully or has instituted or continued proceedings without reasonable cause the defendant's costs should be paid by the prosecutor under section 2 of the Act. If there is any

doubt whether payment will be forthcoming from the prosecutor the position of the defendant should be protected by making an order for costs from central funds in his favour as well.

(b) Where the defendant's own conduct has brought suspicion on himself and has misled the prosecution into thinking that the case against him is stronger than it is the defendant can be left to pay his own costs.

(c) Where there is ample evidence to support a conviction but the defendant is acquitted on a technicality which has no merit. Here again the defendant can be left to pay his own costs.

(d) Where the defendant is acquitted on one charge but convicted on another. Here the court should make whatever order seems just having regard to the relative importance of the two charges and the conduct of the parties generally.

APPENDIX VII

PRONOUNCEMENTS IN COURT

PREFACE

by Lady Ralphs CBE JP DL, Vice President of the Magistrates' Association

The sentence is the focal point of court proceedings for those who have been convicted. For the defendant it may be a turning point, decisive in his whole future. For his fellow citizens its appropriateness is a vital element in that protection without which personal security and public stability are under threat. There can be little doubt that magistrates, at every sitting in every court of the land, can cumulatively enhance attitudes to law and order by the confidence and clarity, calm and courtesy with which they pronounce sentence.

This manual is designed to assist them to have in mind the ingredients essential to each sentence and to encourage them by a suggested form of words which can be adapted according to circumstances. Each case and each defendant is individual and distinct.

Most importantly it is intended as a training manual, preparatory to the task and not to be read from in court. Minimally the justice should be clearly seen to be addressing the defendant and not a paper on his desk. Its value is clear and its usefulness will be ample compensation to the Chairman of the Training Committee (Mrs R E R Thomson) whose initiative it is, and to the Sub-Committee (Mr R H Cozens, Mrs A Tasker and Mr G Whiteside) for patient hours of concentrated hard work.

Enid Ralphs
December 1984

FOREWORD

1. These notes have been prepared by the Magistrates' Association to assist in training court chairmen with the pronouncements that they are most frequently called on to make in court.

2. The essential ingredients of each pronouncement are set out on the left hand pages. A sample wording for each pronouncement is placed on the right hand pages.

3. The sample wordings reflect the Magistrates' Association's

opinion that all pronouncements made in court should not only be legally correct but also readily understandable.

4. Many people who are unfamiliar with court proceedings will have difficulty in understanding the exact meaning of many of the words and phrases so familiar to magistrates. Adjourn, remand, abscond, comply, concurrent, consecutive, recognisance and without reasonable cause are examples. These notes are designed to help court chairmen to avoid using such words and phrases or, where their use is unavoidable, to explain their meaning in simple language.

5. The notes are also designed to encourage the use of the present tense instead of the future tense into which it is so easy to lapse. 'You are fined £100' or 'We fine you £100' are both preferable to, and more accurate than 'You will be fined £100' or 'We will fine you £100'.

6. The Magistrates' Association emphasises that the sample wordings in these notes are merely suggestions for the assistance of court chairmen. In practice it is for each chairman to phrase his pronouncement in the way he deems most suitable for the particular occasion.

7. The ingredients and wordings have been prepared on the assumption that the court clerk is responsible for the speaking parts up to the plea or remand stage.

November 1984
(revised 1986)

CONTENTS

INDEX

INGREDIENTS

No 1

Remand on unconditional bail

1. The date and time when the defendant must return to court.
2. That if the defendant fails to return to court on time on the due date he will be arrested and could subsequently be fined or imprisoned for non-appearance.
3. Does the defendant understand.
4. That the defendant is released on bail.
5. That the defendant will be handed a written bail notice before he leaves the court/building.

PRONOUNCEMENTS

No 1

Remand on unconditional bail

This case cannot be dealt with today. It is being put off until ......
You must come back to this court on .... at .... am/pm

If you do not come on that day at that time you risk being fined or sent to prison.

Do you understand?

Very well, you are granted bail.

As soon as you are handed a written notice about this you may leave the court/building.

INGREDIENTS

No 2

Remand on conditional bail

1. The date and time when the defendant must return to court.
2. The condition(s) on which he is being granted bail, the most common of which are:
   (a) *A surety or sureties.* The amount of the recognisance(s) and the name(s) of the surety(ies).
   (b) *Residential.* The address at which the defendant must reside throughout the period of bail.
   (c) *Curfew.* The times between which the defendant must stay indoors at that address each day.
   (d) *Reporting.* The location of the police station and the time and frequency at which the defendant must report there.
3. The reasons for imposing the condition(s), which may be one or more of the following:
   (a) to ensure that the defendant returns to court on the due date;
   (b) to ensure that the defendant commits no offence while on bail;
   (c) to ensure that the defendant does not interfere with witnesses or otherwise obstruct the course of justice.
4. That if the defendant breaks the condition(s) he will be arrested and may be kept in custody until his case comes to court.
5. That if the defendant fails to return to court on time on the due date he will be arrested and could subsequently be fined or imprisoned.
6. Does the defendant understand.
7. That the defendant will be handed a written bail notice before he leaves the court/building.

PRONOUNCEMENTS

No 2

Remand on conditional bail

This case cannot be dealt with today. It is being put off until ......
The court will release you until then on the following conditions:

(a) that somebody we can trust, that is M...................... will guarantee with money £...... that you will come back.

or

(b) that you must live at .... throughout the period.

or

(c) that you must stay indoors at that address from .... each evening until .... the following morning.

or

(d) that you must report to .... police station each day at .... am/pm.

We are imposing these conditions

(a) so that you will come to court at that time on that day.

or

(b) so that you do not commit an offence in the meantime.

or

(c) so that you will have nothing to do with any of the prosecution witnesses.

If you break any of these conditions you will be arrested and may not be freed until your case comes to court. If you do not come to court at .... am/pm on .... you risk being fined or sent to prison.

Do you understand?

Very well, you are granted bail. As soon as you are handed a written notice about this, you may leave the court/building.

INGREDIENTS

No 3

Obligations of a surety

(The court being already satisfied as to means and reliability)

1. The date and time when the defendant must return to court.
2. That the court requires a surety to be personally responsible for ensuring that the defendant returns to court on time on the due date.
3. The amount of the recognisance into which the surety must enter and which will be forteited if the defendant fails to appear.
4. That the surety must tell the police immediately if he becomes no longer able to ensure the defendant's attendance.
5. Does the proposed surety understand.
6. Is he prepared to stand as surety.
7. That he should sign the appropriate form/book before leaving court.

PRONOUNCEMENTS

No 3

Obligations of a surety

The court is prepared to accept you as a surety in the sum of £.........

You realise that if the defendant does not appear when he is told to then it could mean that you lose your £.........

If you think that the defendant may not come to court as ordered, you should tell the police at once.

Do you understand?

Are you prepared to stand as surety?

Please sign the form/book before you leave the court.

INGREDIENTS

No 4

Remand in custody

1. That the defendant is remanded in custody.
2. The date and time of the adjourned hearing.
3. The exception to the right to bail that the court is applying in this case, there being nine exceptions:

   In imprisonable cases:

   (a) there are substantial grounds for believing that the defendant would fail to surrender to custody.

   (b) there are substantial grounds for believing that the defendant would commit an offence while on bail.

   (c) there are substantial grounds for believing that the defendant would interfere with witnesses or otherwise obstruct the course of justice.

   (d) it has been impracticable to obtain sufficient information about the defendant for the purpose of making a decision.

   (e) it would be impracticable to complete the necessary inquiries without keeping the defendant in custody.

   In non-imprisonable cases:

   (f) having previously been granted bail in criminal proceedings the defendant has failed to surrender to custody and the court believes, in view of that failure, that he would again fail to surrender to custody.

   In all cases:

   (g) the defendant should be in custody for his own protection.

   (h) the defendant is already in custody in pursuance of the sentence of a court.

   (i) having been released on bail in connection with this offence the defendant has been arrested for absconding or breaching the bail conditions.

4. In the case of exception a) or b) or c) the reason for applying the exception, which must be one of the following:

   (a) the nature and seriousness of the alleged offence and the probable sentence for it;

   (b) the character, antecedents and associations, and community ties of the defendant;

   (c) the defendant's response to the granting of bail on previous occasions;

   (d) the strength of the evidence of the defendant having committed the offence.

5. That if the defendant is aggrieved by the decision he may apply for bail

   (a) to a High Court Judge

   or

   (b) if a full bail argument certificate has been given, to the Crown Court.

PRONOUNCEMENTS

No 4

Remand in custody

This case cannot be dealt with today. You are remanded in custody until the morning/afternoon of ....

The court is not granting you bail because

(a) we believe that you would not return to court when required
or
(b) we believe that you would commit an offence while on bail
or
(c) we believe that you would interfere with prosecution witnesses.

Our reasons are:

(i) you are charged with a serious offence which will carry a heavy punishment if you are found guilty.
or
(ii) your character and previous record are not good.
or
(iii) you have not behaved yourself on bail before.
or
(iv) the evidence against you is strong.
or
(v) you have no fixed address.
or
(d) you have failed to answer bail in the past.
or
(e) we need to know more about you before we can decide whether we can grant you bail.
or
(f) you need to be kept in custody for the necessary inquiries to be completed.
or
(g) you should be kept in custody for your own protection.
or
(h) you are already serving a sentence in custody.
or
(i) you have already broken the conditions of bail in this case.

Therefore you will be kept in custody until ....

We have told you our decision. If you still want bail you have the right to apply for it to

(a) a High Court Judge
or
(b) the Crown Court.

INGREDIENTS

No 5

Full bail argument

A certificate that the court has today heard a full argument on the application for bail (following a change of circumstances).

No 6

Future remands in custody in the absence of the defendant

1. The date to which the defendant is remanded in custody.
2. That on that date and on two further occasions the defendant may, if he now consents, be remanded in custody without his personal appearance.
3. That if the defendant consents now, but later changes his mind, he will be brought to court at the next remand hearing or as soon as possible thereafter.
4. Does the defendant understand?
5. Does the defendant consent to being remanded in custody on this basis?

No 7

Remand for social inquiry report

1. That to enable it to reach its final decision the court needs further information about the defendant and the life he leads.
2. That the case will be put off for three/four weeks to enable the probation service to prepare a report containing such information.
3. That the defendant must co-operate with the probation service to enable such a report to be prepared.
4. Continue as for

REMAND ON UNCONDITIONAL BAIL	**1**
or REMAND ON CONDITIONAL BAIL	**2**
or REMAND IN CUSTODY	**4**

PRONOUNCEMENTS

No 5

Full bail argument

The court certifies that it has today heard a full argument on the application for bail (following a change of circumstances).

No 6

Future remands in custody in the absence of the defendant

You are today remanded in custody until ....

On that day and on two further occasions, you may, if you agree, be remanded in custody without being brought to court. If you agree to this now, but later change your mind, you will be brought to court at the next remand hearing or as soon as possible after that.

Do you agree to the court remanding you in custody in your absence as has been explained?

No 7

Remand for social inquiry report

Before the court makes a final decision in your case we need to know more about you. We are therefore asking a probation officer to prepare a report. In the next three/four weeks you must help the probation officer to obtain the information he needs for this. The case is being put off until ....

Continue as for

REMAND ON UNCONDITIONAL BAIL	**1**
or REMAND ON CONDITIONAL BAIL	**2**
or REMAND IN CUSTODY	**4**

INGREDIENTS

No 8

Deferment of sentence

1. The date to which the court proposes to defer passing sentence.
2. The court's expectations of what the defendant will achieve during the deferment.
3. That on that date the court will require information about the defendant's conduct during the period of deferment and about any change in his circumstances.
4. That, if the requisite information is to be presented in the form of a report by a probation officer, the defendant must co-operate with the probation service to enable such a report to be prepared.
5. That if the defendant is convicted of another offence during the period of deferment he may then be sentenced for the present offence.
6. Does the defendant understand?
7. Does the defendant agree to sentencing being deferred?
8. Confirmation of the date and time to which sentencing is deferred.

PRONOUNCEMENTS

No 8

Deferment of sentence

This court is not sentencing you today but will do so on ....

This is to give you an opportunity of

a) making good the damage you have done.
or
b) making progress in your new job.
or
c) settling into your new home.
or
d) ....

On .... the court will want information from a probation officer about your conduct between now and that date and about any change in your circumstances.

You must co-operate with the probation officer to help him prepare his report.

If you are convicted of another offence before .... you may be sentenced at once for today's offence.

Do you understand?

Do you agree to sentencing being deferred?

Sentencing is deferred until ....am/pm on ....

INGREDIENTS

No 9

Absolute discharge

1. That the court grants the defendant an absolute discharge.
2. That this means that, although the defendant is guilty, the court is imposing no penalty.

No 10

Conditional discharge

1. The court discharges the defendant on condition that he commits no further offence for at least the next .... months.
2. That if the defendant does keep out of trouble for that period he will hear nothing further about this offence.
3. That if the defendant is convicted of a further offence committed during that period the defendant can be punished not only for that offence but also for the offence which the court has been considering today.
4. Does the defendant understand?

PRONOUNCEMENTS

No 9

Absolute discharge

The court discharges you absolutely. This means that, although you are guilty, we are not imposing any penalty in this case.

No 10

Conditional discharge

The court discharges you on condition that for the next .... months you keep out of trouble.

This means that you are not being punished for this offence now but if you are convicted of another offence committed during the next .... months you can be punished not only for the new offence but also for the matter we have been considering today.

Do you understand?

INGREDIENTS

No 11

Bind over

1. The period of the proposed order and the amount of the recognisance.
2. The conditions of the order, which are to keep the peace and/or to be of good behaviour towards everybody (and particularly towards a named person).
3. That the breaking of any of these conditions could result in the forfeiture of the recognisance.
4. Does the person understand.
5. Is the person prepared to enter into a recognisance.
6. The order.

PRONOUNCEMENTS

No. 11

Bind over

The court proposes to make an order that you be bound over in the sum of £.......... for a period of .... months/years from today, to keep the peace and to be of good behaviour towards everybody (and in particular towards ....).

This means that if, during the next .... months/years, you break the order you will at the very least, risk having to pay a penalty of £..........

Do you understand?

Do you agree to this order being made?

You are then bound as mentioned in the sum of £..........

INGREDIENTS

No 12

Probation

1. That the circumstances of the offence and the character of the defendant are such that the court may make a probation order instead of imposing a sentence.
2. That the defendant is capable of benefiting from supervision by a probation officer.
3. The period of the probation order that the court is considering.
4. That the court can make such an order only if the defendant agrees to comply with the requirements of the order.
5. The requirements which must include:

   (a) the defendant must be under the supervision of a probation officer, and visit his office when instructed to do so;

   and may include the following, amongst others:

   (b) the defendant must be of good behaviour and lead an industrious life;

   (c) (i) the defendant must notify the probation officer immediately of any change of address and must receive visits from the officer at home,

   or (ii) the defendant must reside at a specified probation hostel;

   (d) The defendant must respond to the advice and guidance of the probation officer.

6. That if the defendant breaks any of these requirements he will be brought back to court and either fined for that breach or dealt with in some other way for the present offence.
7. That if the defendant is convicted of committing a further offence while on probation the probation order may be terminated and some other way found of dealing with him for the present offence.
8. Does the defendant understand.
9. Does the defendant agree to comply with the requirements.
10. The order for the specified period.

PRONOUNCEMENTS

No 12

Probation

Having read the report and considered your circumstances, the court is thinking of making a probation order for .... months/years in your case. This means that, instead of sentencing you now, we will give you the chance to make good by placing you under the supervision of a probation officer for the whole of that period. But we will do this only if you agree to the requirements of such an order, which are that:

(a) you must behave yourself and commit no further offence;

(b) you must keep in touch with the probation officer and see him at his office whenever he tells you to do so;

(c) (i) you must tell the probation officer if you change your address; and you must let him visit you in your own home;

or

(ii) you must live at the .... probation hostel;

(d) you must follow the advice and guidance given by the probation officer.

A probation order does not mean that your offence is being forgotten. If you break any of the requirements of the order, or if you commit a further offence while on probation, you will be brought back to court and could be punished for the offence we have been considering today.

Do you understand?

Do you agree to keep the requirements of the probation order?

Then we make an order for .... months/years.

INGREDIENTS

No 13

Community service

1. That the court is considering making a community service order for a specified number of hours.
2. That this order will require the defendant to give up that amount of his own time during the next twelve months to do unpaid work for the benefit of the community.
3. That the defendant must keep in touch with the probation service, who will tell him where and when to report for work and the kind of work that he will have to do.
4. That the defendant must notify the probation service if he changes his address.
5. That if the defendant does not comply with these terms, or if he fails to work satisfactorily, he will be brought back to court and either fined or dealt with in some other way for the present offence.
6. That if the defendant's circumstances change during the period of the order, either he or the probation service may ask the court to review the order.
7. Does the defendant understand?
8. Does the defendant agree to comply with the terms of the community service order.
9. The order for the specified number of hours.

PRONOUNCEMENTS

No 13

Community service

The court proposes to make a community service order for .... hours.

This means that we are giving you the chance to do something useful, for the benefit of the local community, instead of sentencing you in some other way. You will have to report to the community service organiser when directed, and carry out unpaid work for a total of .... hours during the next 12 months, and in your own time. The organiser will tell you exactly where and when to report, and the kind of work you will have to do. You must tell him straightaway of any change of address.

If you break any of these terms, or do not make a good job of the work you are given, you can be brought back to court and fined or sentenced in some other way for the present offence(s).

You, or the community service organiser, can ask the court to review the order if your circumstances change.

Do you understand?

Do you agree to the order being made?

Then we make a community service order for .... hours.

INGREDIENTS

No 14

Attendance centre

1. The number of hours ordered.
2. The name and address of the attendance centre.
3. The date and time of the defendant's first attendance.
4. That the defendant must attend regularly until he has completed the number of hours ordered.
5. That the defendant will be told when to report to the centre, and must make his own way there at his own expense.
6. That if the defendant misses an attendance, or breaks the rules of the centre, he will be brought back to court and dealt with in some other way for the present offence.
7. Does the defendant understand?

No 15

Detention centre

1. The period of the detention centre order.
2. The reason why the court is of the opinion that no other method of dealing with the defendant is appropriate, which must be one of the following:
   (a) the defendant appears to be unable or unwilling to respond to non-custodial penalties;
   (b) the sentence is necessary for the protection of the public;
   (c) the offence is so serious that a non-custodial sentence cannot be justified.
3. The period of supervision after release.

PRONOUNCEMENTS

No 14

Attendance centre

The court is making an attendance centre order for .... hours. This means that you are to go to the attendance centre at .... Your first attendance will be on Saturday .... at ...... am/pm. You will go regularly until you have completed a total of .... hours there. You will be told how to get to the attendance centre. You are to make your own way there and will pay your own bus or train fares.

If you miss any attendance or do not obey the rules of the attendance centre you may be brought back for the court to punish you in some other way.

Do you understand?

No 15

Detention centre

The court sends you to a detention centre for .... days/weeks.

We consider that there is no other appropriate method of dealing with you because:

(a) it appears that you are unable or unwilling to respond to non-custodial penalties.

or

(b) it is necessary for the protection of the public.

or

(c) the offence is so serious.

When you have served this sentence you will be supervised by a probation officer for the following three months.

INGREDIENTS

No 16

Youth custody

1. The period of the youth custody order.
2. The reason why the court is of the opinion that no other method of dealing with the defendant is appropriate, which must be one of the following:
   (a) the defendant appears to be unable or unwilling to respond to non-custodial penalties;
   (b) the sentence is necessary for the protection of the public;
   (c) the offence is so serious that a non-custodial sentence cannot be justified.
3. If the court is ordering a term of four months or less, its reason for doing so, which must be one of the following:
   (a) the defendant is female;
   (b) the defendant is not fit enough to attend a detention centre;
   (c) the defendant is serving, or has already served, a sentence of imprisonment or detention as a juvenile for a grave crime, or custody for life, or borstal, or youth custody.
4. The period of supervision after release.

PRONOUNCEMENTS

No 16

Youth custody

The court orders you to serve .... days/weeks/months youth custody.

We consider that there is no other appropriate method of dealing with you because

(a) it appears that you are unable or unwilling to respond to non-custodial penalties.

or

(b) it is necessary for the protection of the public.

or

(c) the offence is so serious.

Ordinarily you would serve this sentence in a detention centre but in your case, because:

(a) there is no detention centre for women,

or

(b) of your medical condition,

or

(c) you have served, or are already serving, a sentence of .....
....

you will serve this sentence in a youth custody centre.

When you have served this sentence you will be supervised by a probation officer for at least the following three months.

INGREDIENTS

No 17

Imprisonment for one offence

1. The term of imprisonment.
2. If no previous prison sentence, the reasons why the court is satisfied that no other method of dealing with the defendant is appropriate.

No 18

Imprisonment for more than one offence

1. The identity of each offence and the term of imprisonment being imposed in respect of each one.
2. Whether the terms are consecutive or concurrent.
3. The total period of imprisonment.
4. If no previous prison sentence, the reasons why the court is satisfied that no other method of dealing with the defendant is appropriate.

No 19

Suspension of prison sentence already pronounced

1. The period during which the activation of the sentence(s) is being suspended.
2. That if the defendant commits no further offence during that period he will not have to serve the sentence(s).
3. That if the defendant is convicted of a further offence punishable with imprisonment, and committed during this period of suspension, the court that deals with him for that offence will also have to consider ordering him to serve the sentence(s) imposed today.
4. Does the defendant understand.

PRONOUNCEMENTS

No 17

Imprisonment for one offence

For the offence of .... the court is sending you to prison for .... days/weeks.

No 18

Imprisonment for more than one offence

For the offence of .... the court is sending you to prison for .... days/weeks.

For the offence of .... the court is sending you to prison for .... days/weeks.

These sentences

(a) will be served together, which means that you go to prison for a total of .... days/weeks.

or (b) will be served one after the other, which means that you go to prison for a total of .... days/weeks.

No 19

Suspension of prison sentence already pronounced

This term of imprisonment will be suspended for .... years. This means that if you keep out of trouble for the next .... years you will not have to go to prison. But if during that time you commit another offence punishable with imprisonment, and then are convicted, you can expect to serve the sentence imposed today.

Do you understand?

INGREDIENTS

No 20

Fine, compensation, costs

1. The amount of the fine.
2. The amount of compensation and the reason for awarding it.
3. The costs payable by the defendant.
4. The total amount payable.
5. That this amount is payable through the court.

No 21

Imprisonment in default of fine, following means inquiry (immediate)

1. That the court is satisfied that the default is due to the defendant's wilful refusal or culpable neglect, and that other methods of enforcement are inappropriate or have been unsuccessful.
2. The term of imprisonment.

No 22

Imprisonment in default of fine, following means inquiry (postponed)

1. That the court is satisfied that the default is due to the defendant's wilful refusal or culpable neglect, and that other methods of enforcement are inappropriate or have been unsuccessful.
2. The term of imprisonment.
3. The amount and frequency of the payments that the defendant must make to avoid imprisonment.
4. That the defendant's failure to pay regularly will result in his imprisonment without a further court appearance.
5. Does the defendant understand.

PRONOUNCEMENTS

No 20

Fine, compensation, costs

For the offence of .... the court fines you £.........

You will pay compensation amounting to £.......... in respect of the injury/damage/loss suffered by ....

You will pay costs amounting to £.........

This makes a total of £......... all of which is payable through the court.

No 21

Imprisonment in default of fine, following means inquiry (immediate)

For failing to pay this fine which, in the court's view, you could very well have paid, we are sending you to prison for .... days.

No 22

Imprisonment in default of fine, following means inquiry (postponed)

The court is satisfied that you could have paid this fine. We therefore sentence you to .... days imprisonment, which will not have to be served if you pay at least £..........every week until the debt is cleared.

If you fail to make payment as ordered you will be taken to prison without a further appearance before the court.

Do you understand?

INGREDIENTS

No 23

Attachment of earnings, following means inquiry

1. That the court makes an attachment of earnings order.
2. The normal deduction rate under the attachment of earnings order.
3. That his employer will deduct this amount from each payment of the defendant's wages/salary and send it to the court until the debt is cleared.
4. The protected earnings rate.
5. That the wages/salary payments received by the defendant will not fall below this amount provided that he has earned at least that much.
6. That if the defendant's earnings during any period are too low for the employer to deduct the full normal deduction rate the court will receive a smaller amount.
7. That any shortage in payments to the court will be made good by the deduction of more than the normal deduction rate when the defendant's earnings are higher.
8. That the defendant must inform the court if he changes his employer.
9. Does the defendant understand?

No 24

Disqualification for driving

1. The period of disqualification starting from now.
2. That during this period the defendant must not drive or attempt to drive any motor vehicle on a public road.
3. That if the defendant does so he will be committing an offence which is punishable by imprisonment.
4. Does the defendant understand?

PRONOUNCEMENTS

No 23

Attachment of earnings, following means inquiry

The court is making an attachment of earnings order.

This is an order to your employer requiring him to deduct £......... every week from your wages to be paid to the court. This amount is the normal deduction rate.

Your earnings will be protected up to a figure of £.......... per week. This means that your employer will pay you that amount in full, provided that you have earned that much or more.

If in any week you earn too little for your employer to send the normal £.......... then the court will receive a smaller amount. Any such shortage in payment to the court will have to be made up by larger than normal payments when your earnings are higher.

You must tell the court in writing if you change your employer.

Do you understand?

No 24

Disqualification for driving

You are disqualified for driving for .... months/years from now. This means that you must not drive or attempt to drive any motor vehicle on a public road. If you do so you will be committing an offence for which you could be sent to prison/youth custody.

Do you understand?

INGREDIENTS

No 25

Committal to the Crown Court for trial

1. That the court finds that there is a case for the defendant to answer.
2. That the defendant is committed to the specified Crown Court for trial.
3. That at that trial the defendant may not be permitted to give evidence of an alibi or to call witnesses in support of an alibi unless he has earlier given particulars of that alibi and of any witnesses. He may give those particulars now to the court or at any time during the next seven days to the solicitor for the prosecution at .... police station.
4. Does the defendant understand the alibi warning?
5. That the legal aid for the defendant is extended to cover the trial.
6. That full orders are made for the named witnesses.
7. That conditional orders are made for the named witnesses.
8. That the defendant will be notified of the date and time when he must attend the Crown Court for trial.
9. Continue as for

REMAND ON UNCONDITIONAL BAIL	**1**
REMAND ON CONDITIONAL BAIL	**2**
REMAND IN CUSTODY	**4**

PRONOUNCEMENTS

No 25

Committal to the Crown Court for trial

The court finds that there is a case for you to answer and we commit you to the .... Crown Court for trial by jury.

At that trial you may not be permitted to give evidence of an alibi or call witnesses in support of an alibi unless you have earlier given particulars of that alibi and of the witnesses. You may give those particulars now to the court or at any time during the next seven days to the solicitor for the prosecution at .... police station.

Do you wish to give particulars of an alibi to the court now?

Your legal aid is extended to cover the Crown Court proceedings.

Full orders are made for witnesses

....

....

....

Conditional orders are made for witnesses

....

....

You will be told the date and time when you must go to the Crown Court for your trial.

Continue as for

REMAND ON UNCONDITIONAL BAIL	**1**
REMAND ON CONDITIONAL BAIL	**2**
REMAND IN CUSTODY	**4**

INGREDIENTS

No 26

Committal to the Crown Court for sentence

1. That having now been informed of the defendant's character and antecedents the court considers that its power of dealing with him for this offence is insufficient.
2. That the defendant is committed to the Crown Court for sentence.
3. Does the defendant understand?
4. That the legal aid for the defendant is extended to cover the Crown Court hearing.
5. That the defendant will be notified of the date and time when he must attend the Crown Court for sentence.
6. Continue as for

CUSTODY ON COMMITTAL TO THE CROWN COURT FOR SENTENCE **27**
CONDITIONAL BAIL ON COMMITTAL TO THE CROWN COURT FOR SENTENCE **28**

No 27

Custody on committal to the Crown Court for sentence

1. That the defendant is remanded in custody.
2. That if the defendant is aggrieved by the decision he may apply to the Crown Court for bail.

PRONOUNCEMENTS

No 26

Committal to the Crown Court for sentence

Now that the court has heard about your character and record we think that you deserve a more severe penalty than we can impose. We therefore commit you to the Crown Court for sentence.

Do you understand?

Your legal aid is extended to cover the Crown Court proceedings.

You will be told the date and time when you must go to the Crown Court.

Continue as for

CUSTODY ON COMMITTAL TO THE CROWN COURT FOR SENTENCE **27**

CONDITIONAL BAIL ON COMMITTAL TO THE CROWN COURT FOR SENTENCE **28**

No 27

Custody on committal to the Crown Court for sentence

You are remanded in custody.

If you still want bail you have the right to apply to the Crown Court for it.

INGREDIENTS

No 28

Conditional bail on committal to the Crown Court for sentence

1. That the defendant is released on bail until the date and time when he must attend the Crown Court for sentence, subject to conditions.
2. The condition(s), the most common of which are:
   (a) *A surety or sureties.* The amount of the recognisance(s) and the name(s) of the surety(ies).
   (b) *Residential.* The address at which the defendant must reside throughout the period of bail.
   (c) *Curfew.* The times between which the defendant must stay indoors at that address each day.
   (d) *Reporting.* The location of the police station and the time and frequency at which the defendant must report there.
3. That if the defendant breaks the condition(s) he will be arrested and may be kept in custody until his case comes to court.
4. That if the defendant fails to appear at the Crown Court on time on the due date he will be arrested and could subsequently be fined or imprisoned.
5. Does the defendant understand?
6. That the defendant will be handed a written bail notice before he leaves the court/building.

PRONOUNCEMENTS

No 28

Conditional bail on committal to the Crown Court for sentence

The court will release you until then on the following conditions:

(a) that somebody we can trust will guarantee with money that you will attend the Crown Court when you are told to do so.

or

(b) that you must live at .... throughout the period.

or

(c) that you must stay indoors at that address from .... each evening until .... the following morning.

or

(d) that you must report to .... police station each day at .... am/pm.

If you break any of these conditions you will be arrested and may not be freed until your case comes to court.

If you do not go to the Crown Court when ordered you risk being fined or sent to prison.

Do you understand?

Very well. You are granted bail. As soon as you are handed a written notice about this, you may leave the court/building.

APPENDIX VIII

Checklist for magistrates' search warrants

NOTES ON SEARCH WARRANTS

Golden rules

1. DO NOT DEAL WITH APPLICATIONS UNLESS APPROACHED BY A CLERK
2. ALWAYS ASK APPLICANT FOR IDENTIFICATION
3. IF IN DOUBT – DON'T SIGN – RING A CLERK

<u>The information must:</u>

(a) be in writing
(b) be substantiated on oath
(c) state the grounds of the application
(d) state the relevant statutory authority
(e) specify the premises to be searched
(f) identify (as far as practicable) the articles sought
(g) be signed by the applicant
(h) be signed by the JP and retained by him/her
(i) should be handed to the Justices' Clerk at the earliest opportunity after the grant of the warrant by the JP

<u>Additional Requirements if searching for evidence:</u>

(a) officer has reasonable grounds to believe:
  (i) a **serious arrestable offence** has been committed AND
  (ii) material on the premises of substantial value to the investigation AND
  (iii) material is likely to be **relevant evidence** AND
  (iv) does not consist of items subject to **legal privilege** AND
  (v) does not consist of **excluded material** AND
  (vi) does not consist of **special procedure material**

(b) officer must satisfy you that either

  (i) not practicable to communicate with person entitled to grant entry to the premises OR
  (ii) not practicable to communicate with person entitled to grant access to the evidence OR

Pre-application: Police checks: code of practice		The application: The information		The application: The warrant		Post application: General	
1	Quality of information (i) Accurate	1	In writing, ex parte	1	In writing	1	Any constable may execute warrant
	(ii) Recent	2	On oath	2	Name of applicant	2	Entry and search within one month of issue
	(iii) Not malicious/ irresponsible	3	Grounds of application	3	Date of issue	3	Entry and search at reasonable hour unless purpose would be frustrated
	(iv) Corroborated anonymous	4	Relevant statutory authority	4	Relevant statutory authority	4	Copy of warrant to be handed to occupier
2	Nature of articles sought and their location	5	The premises	5	The premises	5	Executed warrant to be returned to justices' clerk
3	What is known of occupier	6	Articles/persons sought – if possible	6	Articles/persons sought – if possible	6	Warrants returned and retained by court open to inspection by occupier of premises searched
4	Nature of the premises	7	Object of search	7	Signed by JP only		
5	If premises recently searched – how recently		Section 8 applications – searching for evidence. Additional requirements	8	Authorises entry one occasion only		
6	Other relevant information	8	Reasonable grounds for belief	9	Original and two copies clearly marked as such handed to police		
7	Authority of inspector/ senior duty officer	9	Serious arrestable offence	10	Warrant may authorise use by officer of reasonable force if necessary to effect entry		
8	Should local community police officer be consulted	10	Material on premises Of substantial value to investigation Likely to be relevant evidence – not concluded				
		11	and not able to contact person entitled to grant entry to premises				
		12	or able to contact etc, but not able to contact person entitled to grant access to evidence				
		13	or entry will be refused				
		14	or purpose may be frustrated or seriously prejudiced by giving notice				
		15	all information signed by applicant and JP and retained by court				

(iii) entry will not be granted to premises unless warrant produced OR
(iv) purpose of search will be frustrated or seriously prejudiced by giving notice of the search

The warrant must:

(a) be in writing
(b) name the applicant
(c) contain the date of issue
(d) state the relevant statutory authority
(e) name the premises
(f) name the articles sought if possible
(g) state any persons authorised to accompany a constable executing the warrant
(h) be signed by the JP

If you grant the warrant:

(a) the original, and TWO copies marked COPY should be handed to the police. The copies should also be signed
(b) warrant may authorise a constable to use reasonable force to effect an entry
(c) authorises one entry only
(d) entry and search must be within one month from the date of its issue
(e) entry and search must be at a reasonable hour unless this would frustrate the purpose of the search
(f) copy of warrant to be handed to the occupier of the premises, or in his absence another person who appears to be in charge of the premises. If no person is present a copy shall be left at the premises
(g) after execution shall be endorsed as to when executed and what if anything was found, and then returned to the Justices' Clerks' office where it may be inspected by the occupier of the premises.

Index